THE ART OF THE STEAL

Trump and the Economic Hit Man Presidency

JOHN PERKINS

Berrett-Koehler
PUBLISHERS

Berrett-Koehler Publishers, Inc.
1333 Broadway, Suite P100
Oakland, CA 94612-1921
(510) 817-2277
bkconnection.com

Ordering Information
Quantity sales. Special discounts are available on quantity purchases by corporations, associations, individuals, and others. For details, please go to bkconnection.com to see our bulk discounts or contact bookorders@bkpub.com for more information.
Textbook exam/desk copies. Please consult the General FAQ at bkconnection.com.
Bookstore orders for trade or textbook use. For print books, please contact Penguin Random House Publisher Services at customerservice@penguinrandomhouse.com. For ebooks, contact your favorite distributor.
Distributed to the US trade and internationally by Penguin Random House Publisher Services.

The authorized representative in the EU for product safety and compliance is EU Compliance Partner, Pärnu mnt. 139b-14, 11317 Tallinn, Estonia, www.eucompliancepartner.com, +372 5368 65 02.

Printed in the United States of America

Berrett-Koehler books are printed on long-lasting acid-free paper. When it is available, we choose paper that has been manufactured by environmentally responsible processes. These may include using trees grown in sustainable forests, incorporating recycled paper, minimizing chlorine in bleaching, or recycling the energy produced at the paper mill.

Library of Congress Cataloging-in-Publication Data
Names: Perkins, John, 1945- author
Title: The art of the steal : Trump and the economic hit man presidency / John Perkins.
Description: Oakland, CA : Berrett-Koehler Publishers, Inc, [2026] | Includes bibliographical references and index.
Identifiers: LCCN 2026012675 (print) | LCCN 2026012676 (ebook) | ISBN 9798890572554 paperback | ISBN 9798890572561 pdf | ISBN 9798890572578 epub
Subjects: LCSH: United States—Economic policy—2009- | Trump, Donald, 1946-
Classification: LCC HC106.84 .P44 2026 (print) | LCC HC106.84 (ebook)
LC record available at https://lccn.loc.gov/2026012675
LC ebook record available at https://lccn.loc.gov/2026012676

First Edition

35 34 33 32 31 30 29 28 27 26 10 9 8 7 6 5 4 3 2 1

Book production: Happenstance Type-O-Rama
Cover design: Ashley Ingram

To the courageous people who have opposed,
continue to oppose, and will oppose autocratic
leaders and oligarchs around the world.

Contents

Introduction

The Hit Man Comes Home

THIS BOOK IS NOT just about Donald J. Trump. Yes, his name appears throughout these pages and in the subtitle. But he is merely a symbol of how the economic hit man (EHM) strategy has evolved, regardless of which political party occupies the White House. It has taken over the US presidency.*

Other countries are led by economic hit men, including the two with the largest nuclear arsenals after the United States: Russia and China. However, the United States is unique in that it has served as a beacon for democracy during most of the past 250 years. The other countries have long histories of governments that are openly autocratic.

When I wrote the first edition of *Confessions of an Economic Hit Man* in 2004, I never expected to see the techniques I'd used in distant countries deployed so openly inside my own country—and by the US government itself. I never imagined that the beacon of democracy could be eclipsed by the dark veil of oligarchy. I never guessed that a US president would openly praise and mimic autocrats like Russia's Putin, China's Xi, and Hungary's Orbán.

---

* Although the generic term is economic hit *man*, women also play that role.

That book exposed a strategy that operated in the shadows behind the beacon. It created a system that is backed by powerful corporate, financial, and political interests. Our economic hit man tools included fraudulent financial reports, inflated promises, questionable elections, manufactured fears, corruption, coercion, sex, threats of retribution, and even assassinations. The goal was to control the planet's resources and funnel money into the coffers of huge corporations and the pockets of a few wealthy families. It was the art of the steal painted as legitimate.

In the years since, the economic hit man system has metastasized. It no longer limits itself to economically vulnerable nations. It has also turned inward. As president, Trump has mastered the art of the steal and displayed it for all to see.

Trump's frequent dismissal of scientific consensus, hostility toward experts, and politicization of education and research has taken a toll on institutions that every previous administration has championed. He rejects a principle that was established in the United States 250 years ago—that progress is driven by rational debate and evidence-based decision-making. His leadership style emphasizes loyalty over law and strength over cooperation. His aggressive nationalism, public threats toward other nations, and withdrawal from multilateral agreements demonstrate a preference for domination and unilateral action rather than shared global problem-solving.[1]

Trump defined the nature of his economic hit man presidency during the first day of his second term as president. On January 20, 2025, he granted blanket clemency to the nearly sixteen hundred people convicted of or awaiting trial for assault and other crimes committed during the January 6, 2021, attack on the US Capitol. At least 140 police officers were injured, and one later died. A number of other officers died by suicide in the months following the incident.

Although those clemencies and the many actions that followed in 2025 shocked the world, they were superseded during the first weeks of 2026. In the first and second months of the second year of Trump's second term, he took actions that raised global outrage: deploying a massive military force into Venezuela, sending thousands of heavily armed federal troops to Minneapolis, threatening to take over Greenland, and attacking Iran.

Trump justified the Venezuelan operation as necessary for ending the rule of the country's self-proclaimed president. He justified the Minneapolis operation by threatening to invoke the Insurrection Act and calling people who protested the killing of US citizens by ICE agents "domestic terrorists." He justified his determination to own Greenland as part of his national defense strategy, claiming that US control is essential to counter Russian and Chinese interests in the Arctic.[2]

It soon became apparent that these were more than attempts to overthrow a government, disperse protesters, and occupy territory. They were dramatic symbols of the president's use of the EHM strategy: When economic tactics fail, send in the jackals.

Trump highlighted his willingness to use jackal tactics when, on February 28, 2026, he joined Israel's Netanyahu in launching a major military attack against Iran. He asserted that it and the war that followed were necessary to protect the United States against Iranian nuclear weapons. This contradicted his earlier assertion that Iran's nuclear enrichment facilities had been obliterated by US military strikes in June 2025. It also contradicted Secretary of Defense Pete Hegseth's claims that Iran's nuclear ambitions had been destroyed.

I met with business leaders in New York City the day after airstrikes killed Iran's supreme leader Khamenei. They were very worried about the negative impacts this war was likely to have on US businesses, supply chains, and the global economy. One asked, "How can a United States president who so actively sought the Nobel Peace Prize in 2025 be so belligerent in 2026?" Another responded, "Trump thinks he's America's new king."

In the following weeks, their worries turned out to be well founded. The Iranians closed the Strait of Hormuz, shutting down about 20 percent of the world's oil supply, negatively impacting economies everywhere, and causing political chaos in many countries. When Trump demanded that NATO countries and other allies join the United States in the fight against Iran and force the reopening of the strait, they refused. They pointed out that the US president had launched the attack without consulting them—or his own Congress. Trump threatened to pull the United States out of NATO, an action that would severely undermine America's security and economic interests.

I recalled the time I'd spent in Bandar Abbas on the Strait of Hormuz in the 1970s. The company I served as chief economist, Chas. T. Main Inc. (MAIN), was hired by the shah (with the Pentagon's blessings) to help develop a military base there that gave the shah, and presumably the United States, control over this strategic waterway. It turned out to be a terrible mistake. Today, Bandar Abbas is the location of Iran's First Naval Zone, major ports, and branches of the Islamic Revolutionary Guard Corps. And they have shut down the strait.

The US military has known ever since I worked in Iran fifty years ago that whoever controls Bandar Abbas controls the Strait of Hormuz. I assume that the Pentagon and CIA have shared that knowledge with Trump. I have to wonder how Washington could have blundered into this war without taking out Bandar Abbas. The initial US attacks may have killed Iran's leadership, but they failed to disarm one of the most critical military bases in the world. It also seems absurd for a US president to demand that our European allies face the consequences without us. After all, the United States started this war, and the US economy is vulnerable to global oil prices.

Regardless of the final outcome, the war in Iran has undermined US credibility around the world. Trump and other members of his administration have frequently made threats and given ultimatums—and then backed down. Neither Iran nor NATO and other traditional US allies have confidence that Washington will honor any agreements or commitments it makes. Furthermore, the expenditure of military and financial resources in Iran has eroded US commitments to Ukraine in its war against Russia—a war Trump had promised to end in the first day of his second term.

Trump's shows of extreme force send a message across the world that he, like kings and emperors of the past, thinks he has the power to do whatever he wants. That message serves as a warning to US citizens and leaders everywhere: Play the US's economic hit man game or else . . .

Those actions will define Trump's place in history.

Whether you voted for Trump or not, whether you love him or hate him, you'll have to agree that he has shaken us up. He has invigorated American politics. Just about everyone is talking about him. Those who support him say he is "draining the swamp" and "putting America first." Those who oppose him say he is "a dictator, supporting an oligarchy" and "turning the world against us." One thing is for certain: He has exposed flaws in the system of checks and balances that I, for one, was raised to believe protected us in the United States from the horrors we had witnessed in other countries. China, Russia, and other repressive governments were expected to have autocratic leaders. But not the United States.

THE EVOLUTION OF AN OLIGARCHY

This book is **not** about partisan politics. All US presidents since Dwight D. Eisenhower and John F. Kennedy—Democrat and Republican alike—have relied on the modern version of economic hit men to execute their policies. But Trump is the first to master the art himself. He is the first president to use the presidency to enrich himself openly and shamelessly and to engage in corrupt practices in full view of the media and the public.

This book **is** about the evolution of an oligarchy-led corporatocracy and its economic hit men. It details the ways their methods have been adapted for domestic consumption. Although Trump did not invent these tactics, he amplified them, branded them, and adjusted them to fit his personality. He has become the embodiment of the economic hit man presidency.

Trump is the product of a changing world and a symbol of how an economic hit man can rise through the ranks to become the most influential man on the planet. Unfortunately, his economic hit man presidency has also supported and encouraged autocratic movements on every continent. And it remains to be seen how Trump's example is influencing the young people who will become our future leaders.

During the majority of the ten years when I was an economic hitman, I believed in what I was doing. I was like the bully who concludes that because people give in to him, he must be right. Once I finally understood how wrong I was and how terribly destructive the economic hit man system was, I had a hard time getting out. There were tremendous pressures to stay in. In addition, there were many perks—flying first class around the world, meeting with heads of state, staying in five-star hotels, wining and dining in the finest restaurants, receiving a great salary. I was living a life that the son of a New Hampshire schoolteacher had previously only seen in movies and dreams.

As I've detailed in earlier books, I wavered. I wanted to believe those who sought to convince me that I was doing good. I wanted to continue to enjoy the perks. But my conscience knew better. I suffered through nightmares and pangs of guilt. Increasingly, I saw the world I was helping to create as one that was dangerously divided, constantly on the brink of devastating wars, consuming and polluting itself toward its own destruction.

It took me longer than it should have, but after three years of wavering, I finally broke the chains and quit. It took more years before I committed to exposing the economic hit man world and working to change it.

My intent in writing this book is to highlight the methods I and other economic hit men used over the years and compare and contrast them with those being applied in the United States and other countries right now. Although economic hit men come from many different backgrounds, they share a strategy that enables them to change the policies and the basic character of the countries they dominate. As I write this book, Trump has entered the second year of his second term as president and has already used this strategy to radically reshape this country—and the way the rest of the world judges us.

HOLDING THE POWER

Some dismiss Trump as a buffoon.

I do not agree.

He is impetuous, shoots from the hip, and makes decisions without thinking far ahead. It reminds me of what I was told after I passed my first black belt test in martial arts many years ago.

"You've learned all the basic techniques and skills," my teacher assured me. "Now you get to use them without thinking. When you spar, rely on your instincts."

Trump's life has been one of learning the basic techniques and skills of the extremely brutal and competitive real estate business in New York City. He's had to deal with shrewd businessmen, vicious racketeers, aggressive politicians, and manipulative financers. He's been burned, made mistakes, and filed for bankruptcy more than once—and yet he's managed to win the presidency. Twice. He may play the buffoon at times. That just might be his greatest asset.[3]

I recall my first assignment in Indonesia in 1971. The evening before my initial meeting with a top government official, I was visited by a "commercial officer" from the US embassy (a position I later learned is often filled by CIA agents). He told me he'd heard that I was nervous about the meeting and asked why.

"I'm terrified that I'll make a fool of myself," I said. "I don't think I know the language or how to deal with someone who is so much more knowledgeable and experienced than me."

"Look," he responded. "If that happens, rub your chin slowly, frown menacingly, and say something like, 'I understand that, but . . .' squint and give him an intimidating stare, 'I need more details.' Never admit you don't know. Act like you hold the power." He gave me a conspiratorial grin. "Remember, it's all about perception. Your job is to convince Indonesia to accept a huge loan. The man you're meeting with and his family and friends will get rich off it. He wants to believe you. Make him believe you."

That advice gave me an insight that I have never forgotten. The art of the steal involves convincing people that serving their short-term personal ambitions is doing the right thing, even when they know in their hearts that what they are doing is wrong, that they are being lied to and are lying to themselves and others.

Trump applies that art masterfully. He convinces people to take actions in the short term that are detrimental in the long run, such as investing heavily in fossil fuels rather than in sustainable energy sources. He persuades Republicans to applaud his campaign promises to keep the country out of wars and then, once in the White House, convinces them to support huge taxpayer-funded military build-ups in the Caribbean and Middle East, followed by massive attacks on Venezuela and Iran that increase oil prices and disrupt global supply chains.

Trump doesn't have to think long-term. He's been handed the blueprints. During his first term, he was guided by comprehensive schemes developed by Steve Bannon, Stephen Miller, and others. They provided him with early "action plans" of executive orders intended to send a shock-and-awe signal that this president was rapidly fulfilling his campaign promises. All he had to do was frown menacingly, stare intimidatingly, never admit to being wrong, and act like he held the power. Perception.

In the first year of his second term, the president relied heavily on Project 2025, a comprehensive, meticulously developed plan from the Heritage Foundation, a conservative think tank. It provided a "Mandate for Leadership" game plan as well as an implementation playbook. Its goals included strengthening presidential authority over agencies, rolling back regulations, reducing the size and scope of the federal government, and advancing traditional conservative positions on issues like abortion, diversity and equity rights, and immigration.

Like any good economic hit man, Trump can fall back on the instincts and tactics he developed over many years in the trenches. He can shoot from the hip and make unscripted—often controversial—comments, as long as he follows the playbook. He is like the front-line general executing the battle plan devised by his strategists.

In the process, he has undermined the American Ideal.

THE AMERICAN/GLOBAL IDEAL

Over the years, I've traveled to and worked in many countries. In 2025 I spoke at events in Asia, Europe, and Latin America. Everywhere I go, I meet people who love the American Ideal: a set of principles that promote liberty with responsibility, equality, justice, democracy, opportunity, and an individualism that also supports and strengthens family and community.

China may offer a seductive economic model. In less than twenty years, it has replaced the United States as the number one trading partner in nearly three-quarters of the world's countries. But most people who dream of leaving their homelands want to come here, not there.[4]

Unlike China, Russia, and other autocracies, the United States was founded on the belief that "all men are created equal" and endowed "with certain unalienable Rights, that among these are Life, Liberty, and the pursuit of Happiness." Ever since those principles were set out in the Declaration of Independence 250 years ago, this country has been their standard bearer. Now the standard bearer is marching in a different direction and trampling on the standard—and that impacts the entire world.

The country has never fully realized its lofty ideals. Trump's economic hit man presidency has made it clear that we have failed to remove the possibility of autocracy in this country. The American Revolution freed us from the British monarchy, and now we stand at another crossroads: Do we head down the path symbolized by the Statue of Liberty's torch of democracy, or do we continue into the dark shadows of an economic hit man presidency? In the cries of the "No Kings" rallies that stretch across the land, we hear the answer.

We in the United States have an opportunity to regain the status of revered leader that we enjoyed for several decades following World War II, before we fell under the spell of the economic hit man system.

Trump's first term and the beginning of his second term have already established that this era will not be a footnote to history. Something radical has happened in the United States, something we have never witnessed before, something that has set the world on a new course.

One of this book's goals is to offer current and future generations a look at how this radical change evolved. Trump's strategy grew out of our successful economic hit man experiments in the 1970s. Presidents have expanded and enhanced that strategy ever since. Trump has taken it to levels that we never could have imagined in my day.

Perhaps the greatest gift Trump has given us is to shake us awake to our potential and our need to change.

If those who love Trump and those who hate him can agree that he has exposed deep flaws in our system, we can commit to redirecting our energies toward repairing those flaws, manifesting the American Ideal, and offering a new model to the world that reflects universal human desires—a Global Ideal.

REROUTING THE FUTURE

In the following pages, I do not attempt to list all the things Trump has already done or anticipate what might happen next in his second term. The former would be overwhelming and the latter pure speculation. Rather, I provide an overview of the ways he has employed tactics that I once used. For me, the goal was to steal the resources of and gain control over other countries. He has that same goal, plus another: to control the United States in a way that is beyond anything experienced by any previous president, and to add billions of dollars to his family's coffers.[5] His system is built on the four pillars of the EHM strategy I helped develop: fear, debt, anxiety over scarcity, and divide and conquer. This strategy is also used by China's Xi, Russia's Putin, and other autocrats.

Although he claims to have mastered the art of the deal, what Trump has truly mastered is the art of the steal. He has established the four pillars of the EHM strategy as the foundations for his policies and actions.

This book is a warning. But more than that, it is a call to action and a blueprint for creating a different future. In my previous books, I've written that the EHM strategy has created a degenerative Death Economy that is consuming and polluting itself toward extinction. The challenge now is to replace that with a regenerative Life Economy that restores, rejuvenates, and recycles. The American Ideal offers a model for a Global Ideal that can make that happen.

Chapters 1 and 2 provide essential background; they introduce the four pillars and focus on the major themes, including the evolution and current significance of the EHM strategy. Chapters 3 through 7 describe each of the four pillars in detail, my personal experiences as an economic hit man, and the way Trump has applied and expanded the tactics I helped develop. Chapter 8 and the Conclusion are the heart of this book. They explore the role of perception in creating reality and offer a blueprint for change, a plan of action that each of us can take to turn things around.

By the time you read this, things certainly will have changed, probably a great deal. Trump will have added many twists and turns, but the route has been mapped. This is a guidebook on how we reverse it.

AUTHOR'S NOTE ON NOTES

The notes at the back of this book include more information than appears in the note superscript pop-up windows in e-books. Please find the entire notes in the Notes section at the end of the book.

1

Evolution of the Economic Hit Man System

I SPENT MY ECONOMIC HIT MAN years promoting corporate, governmental, and covert systems that claim to improve global prosperity and support democracy. However, once stripped of their marketing gloss, these systems amount to a form of colonization that expands influence, extracts wealth, and controls nations and their people. The language changes. But the underlying objective—domination masked as benevolence—persists.

When I first entered the economic hit man ranks in 1971, I believed I was serving a noble cause. After graduating from business school in 1968, I'd been stationed as a Peace Corps volunteer deep in the Amazon rainforest and high in the Andes Mountains of Ecuador. As Chapter 6 will describe, my assignment was to help poor people rise from the depths of severe poverty.

After my tour ended in late 1970, I was recruited by Chas. T. Main Inc. (MAIN), a low-profile, high-impact, Boston-based consulting firm that did a lot of business with the World Bank, International Monetary Fund (IMF), US Treasury Department, and many foreign governments, as well as US corporations. Prior to joining the Peace Corps, I had been recruited by the National Security Agency (NSA) and passed a series of security clearance and other tests. At MAIN, I was told that my education and the survival, language, and cultural sensitivity skills I'd developed in Ecuador qualified me for the job as an economist (and, within eighteen months, chief economist). It was, I believed, the logical next step toward my Peace Corps goal of ending poverty.

The early 1970s were the height of the Cold War, and I soon discovered that I'd been hired to implement a US strategy in Africa, Asia, Latin America, and the Middle East that would stop Communism. We told the world—and ourselves—that we were helping impoverished nations and encouraging democracy. In fact, we were making the rich and powerful richer and more powerful as well as increasing human inequality, environmental destruction, and species extinctions. This strategy caused a great deal of resentment in countries that were victimized by it.

Although we did not fully understand it until after Trump's inauguration in 2017, the strategy also encouraged Russian and Chinese leaders to follow in the footsteps of their former ruthless dictators, Stalin and Mao. Ironically, when Trump reduced the US foreign service and foreign aid and pulled us out of major international organizations, he helped to facilitate Russia's and China's goal of dominating the world.[6]

In my book *Confessions of an Economic Hit Man*, I've described my job this way:

> *I walked into the office of a leader in a country that had just discovered it had lots of oil. I told him, "Our construction companies will rent equipment from your brother's John Deere franchise. We'll pay twice the going rate." The implication was that his brother would share his profits with him. I went on to explain that we'd make similar deals with friends of his who owned Coca-Cola bottling plants, other food and beverage suppliers, and labor contractors. We'd see to it that his children, and those of his family and closest friends, would be accepted into great American colleges, and we'd give them full scholarships. All he had to do was sign off on a World Bank loan that would hire US*

corporations to build infrastructure projects in his country and would bury his people in debts they could never repay. These were outright bribes—and perfectly legal under US laws.

Then I casually mentioned that refusing would bring in the jackals.

"Remember," I said, "what happened to . . ." I rattled off a list of names like Mossadegh of Iran, Árbenz of Guatemala, Allende of Chile, Lumumba of Congo, Diem of Vietnam. "All of them," I said, "were overthrown or"—I ran a finger across my neck—"because they didn't play our game."

We made it easy for leaders to succumb to what became known as the "debt trap."

I must admit that I often questioned the morality of my actions. However, my training in business school and the Peace Corps, as well as most of the literature generated by the US educational system and institutions like the World Bank and United Nations, convinced me that I was doing the right thing. These institutions maintain that lending countries large sums of money—collateralized by their oil or other natural resources—and using that money to hire our own companies to build electric power systems, highways, ports, and other infrastructure projects in those countries generate spectacular economic growth. As will become clear in upcoming pages, this is an extremely deceptive conclusion based on statistics that are biased toward the rich and powerful.

Once I bought into the system, it was difficult to get out. I tried to quit several times but succumbed to extreme pressure and stayed in for an additional three years. Each time, I convinced myself that our work was good work, even though I knew in my heart that it was not. As MAIN's president Chuck Noble, a retired army major general, told me, "Doing the right thing sometimes requires compromise. Winning a war means that you've got to sacrifice certain principles, lose battles, and then—victory." In addition to all the convincing arguments, I'd grown up the son of an underpaid teacher in a boarding school filled with very rich boys. Now finally I was making a great salary and, like those boys, traveling first class around the world.

A cartoon that was popular when I was a kid shows Bugs Bunny pondering a decision. An angel sits on one shoulder, urging him to make the moral choice. The devil sits on his other shoulder, offering all kinds of perks if he does the opposite. In my experience, the devil can be terribly seductive and often disguises himself as an angel. My devil promised me the American dream.

Anthropologists tell us that humans have a history of following a strong leader during times of crisis. We may not consider the moral issues, or whether this leader is devil or angel. Instead, we simply follow someone who promises to deliver us from the crisis. Although many people did not consider the United States to be in crisis during the Biden administration, Trump kept insisting that we were. And, according to his campaign promises, he was the only person who could pull us out. He would "make America great again."

Today, the economic hit man system has mutated into something far more pervasive and sophisticated than it was on my watch. Even more ominously, it brings the exploitation home. What once targeted distant presidents and ministers now aims squarely at US residents, in addition to those in other nations. A new breed of economic hit men that had entered the scene before Trump took office had learned that the same techniques used to persuade foreign officials to sell out their nations could be applied to the American people themselves.

Trump has become the ringleader of this newly emerging economic hit man gang. He shamelessly advocates actions that would have been considered immoral, dishonorable, and even illegal in my time. He presents them in a fool's gold cloak of "making America first" when in fact they are doing the exact opposite.

To understand Trump's role in this evolution, we must understand the system that shaped him—and that he, in turn, has augmented.

THE FIRST WAVE: EXTERNAL EMPIRE

In the decades following World War II, the United States emerged as a global superpower not because its military was the largest, but because it pioneered an economic variant of empire that was subtler, more palatable, and much more efficient than military conquest.

The strategy began with the Marshall Plan, a highly successful approach aimed at helping Europe recover from the devastation of World War II and preventing the spread of Communism. It invested more than $13 billion in programs that strengthened Western Europe's economies and political stability and created markets for American goods and services. Primarily financed through grants, rather than loans, it could have served as a model for future strategies in the rest of the world. However, the Marshall Plan ended in 1951, a time when the Korean War was shifting US foreign aid priorities from economic recovery to military assistance.

The World Bank, IMF, and their sister organizations took up where the Marshall Plan left off, with a major difference: Their work was mostly financed not through grants but by interest-bearing loans collateralized with the client country's natural resources.

This created the perfect tool for the "first wave" of economic hit men, the debt-trap economists. As described in the original *Confessions*, World Bank loans targeted lower-income, resource-rich nations. Our weapons included deceptive reports backed by sophisticated computer models, and infrastructure projects that funneled wealth into corporations—all under the banner of "constructive development."

Countries from Ecuador to Indonesia found themselves caught in webs of debt they could never repay. We demanded the collateral. Resources flowed outward to the creditor countries' corporations. Inequality deepened. However, due to the highly effective propaganda from the World Bank and other institutions, the perception remained intact: The United States was the benevolent savior that led the world toward prosperity.

THE SECOND WAVE: EMPIRE COMES HOME

By the early 2000s, the system began turning inward. Policies once imposed on distant nations through institutions like the World Bank and IMF began appearing in the United States. These included deregulations that favored corporations over communities, privatization of public services and lands, austerity for the many, subsidies for the powerful, and a propaganda machine that sold inequality as freedom.

In *The New Confessions*, I warned that the EHM strategy was no longer confined to the developing world. It had become domestic policy. Corporate economic hit men, including lobbyists, consultants, lawyers, investment bankers, and compromised politicians and government officials, were conditioning Americans to accept the same illusions we had once crafted for foreign leaders: that short-term profit was prosperity, that corporate dominance was democracy, that environmentally destructive extraction was progress.

This was the soil in which Donald Trump's political persona took root and grew.

THE THIRD WAVE: CHINA'S CHALLENGE

By the time China's EHM strategy surged across the globe—its New Silk Road replacing US dominance in many regions—I recognized an emerging pattern. As described in detail in the third edition of *Confessions*, China had taken the model the United States crafted, refined it, and then projected it outward with astonishing speed. The contest for global influence had shifted from battlefields to boardrooms and from overt threats to subtle manipulations of perception. One telling statistic: In 2001, the United States was the number one trading partner for 80 percent of the world's countries, but by 2023 China had taken that position for 70 percent of the world's countries.[7]

Here at home, something equally unprecedented was happening. Americans were electing leaders who did not challenge the corporatocracy; they *represented* it. They were building an unsustainable Death Economy.

2

The Homeland Hit Man

TRUMP DID NOT INVENT the forces that shaped him. He mastered them. His business practices, public image, and political ascent make it clear to me that he had learned to manipulate his own people, as well as foreign heads of state, by applying economic hit man tactics.

In my job, I convinced others to act against their long-term interests by appealing to emotion over fact, fear over reason, illusion over reality. I and others with similar jobs operated by promising affluence while obscuring the costs. We used fear, debt, deception, and division to concentrate power upward. We manufactured crises and presented ourselves as the only solution.

What's referred to as "the rental economy" has also become a subtle form of debt. We rent many of the things we used to own. We rent computer programs, music, movies, the internet, and so many other aspects of life on a monthly basis. We don't own them. If we don't make the monthly payments, we lose them. In other words, we are in constant debt to many of the goods and services that are an integral part of our lives.

When Donald Trump and his wife, Melania, descended the famous golden escalator in the atrium of Trump Tower in New York

City on June 15, 2015, to announce his candidacy for president in the 2016 election, he wasn't merely launching a political campaign; he was delivering a classic economic hit man pitch.

Trump followed the economic hit man playbook to the letter. He promised to increase prosperity by reducing the cost of living and decreasing taxes. His slogan "Make America Great Again" was a promise to bring peace to the world, end US meddling in foreign politics, and create jobs for Americans by supporting US manufacturing industries and deporting immigrants. The latter, he said, would drastically reduce crime.

Trump echoed the economic hit man claims that only we (he) could accomplish these things, that he was the master at cutting deals, and his deals would benefit America. It was a pivotal moment that launched the MAGA movement and changed American politics.

PERCEPTION MOLDS REALITY

Marketing executives, psychotherapists, politicians, and military and intelligence psychological operations (PSYOPs) experts all know that perception drives actions that mold reality. Countries, cultures, religions, and corporations do not exist until enough people accept a perception that inspires them to take reality-altering actions.

Perception is the keystone of the EHM strategy for dominating other nations—and it has become the currency of modern American politics. Trump understands this intuitively. He built a career by branding illusion as reality. His image as a successful tycoon was manufactured by his propagandists, the TV show *The Apprentice*, and the ghostwriter of *Trump: The Art of the Deal.* The details and facts don't matter; the image does.

People who feel abandoned by the system are desperate for a perceived champion. They are vulnerable to narratives that promise restoration to the "good old days," superiority, or revenge. They are susceptible to the myth of the savior who alone can solve their problems. In my days, we told heads of state that our projects could save their countries from humiliation and collapse.

Trump mastered the domestic variant. As early as 1987, when *The Art of the Deal* was first published, his writings reflected his understanding of the power of forging perceptions that served his goals. Here are a couple of examples from that book that are right out of the economic hit man handbook:

> *People want to believe that something is the biggest and the greatest and the most spectacular.*
>
> *The final key to the way I promote is bravado. I play to people's fantasies. . . . I call it truthful hyperbole. It's an innocent form of exaggeration—and a very effective form of promotion.*[8]

Long before he officially ran for president, Trump began to shape his campaign rhetoric. He proclaimed that the world was ripping us off; China was determined to engulf us; Europe was exploiting our military; India was dumping its goods in our markets; immigrants were coming here to steal from us, rape our women, and destroy our social fabric; and environmental and climate change activists were conspiracy theorists determined to eviscerate our economy. It would, he claimed, take a dominant leader—him—to turn things around.

His message wasn't political rhetoric. It was an economic hit man message delivered on a national scale. Donald Trump excels at delivering messages that promote his interests.

Every economic hit man operation begins with control over perception. This means crafting economic projections and detailed studies that convince leaders of what they want to hear and producing fancy reports that purport to offer explosive growth, endless prosperity, and prestige on the global stage. The numbers don't need to be true; they only need to be believable. They need to justify huge debts.

One of the jobs that bothered my conscience the most was that of presenting an unelected hierarchy of CEOs, financiers, lobbyists, consultants, media barons, and intelligence-linked contractors as a natural extension of democracy. In fact, I suspected that it was the emergence of an American oligarchy. Despite my own misgivings, I convinced myself that I had a job to do and that better minds than mine had determined that the ends justified the means, that our system would ultimately create a more just and democratic world. I conveyed this false perception to the top decision-makers in countries like Ecuador, Guatemala, and Iran, where autocratic governments were striving to portray themselves as democratic.

"In America," I bragged, "the poorest born can rise to the top." It was the rags-to-riches story in the extreme. Although true of some US presidents, including Lincoln and Truman, I knew it was also true of dictators like Stalin and Mussolini. In the early years, I convinced myself that this story was promoting democracy. Once I understood otherwise, I was in so deep, it was hard to dig out. I stopped repeating it, but I couldn't go back and change what the lies had already accomplished. I would wake up in the middle of the night drenched in sweat, haunted by what I'd done. I would then quote to myself the words of Shakespeare's Lady Macbeth: "What's done is done" and "What's done cannot be undone."

Don't look back, just keep moving forward.

Those thoughts helped me live with myself. And yet . . . it also struck me that Lady Macbeth was justifying murder. Eventually, those thoughts would motivate me to write books that expose the EHM strategy and advocate for change.

The false narrative that oligarchy is natural to and symbolic of democracy has turned out to be one of the most effective economic hit man tools. Freedom of speech, the narrative claims, gives individuals the right to lie and cheat their way into Congress and the White House. A corrupted system allows corporations to buy politicians through campaign financing.

As I look back at the days when I peddled such lies and woke up covered in sweat, I wonder how disseminating that narrative impacts the people today who work for the oligarchs—the administrators, accountants, lawyers, lobbyists, chiefs of staff, and publicists. Do they suffer from nightmares like I did? How do they justify continuing in their jobs?

By the early 2000s, the false perception had become pervasive; the economic hit man system had grown more distributed, more networked, and more sophisticated. It no longer required individuals like me to deliver the message, face to face. The new economic hit men worked for multinational corporations, private equity firms, data-mining platforms, and those who manipulated currencies, interest rates, and algorithms. Supreme Court rulings like *Citizens United* in 2010 not only gave corporations and their owners incredible power but also indicated that the courts were willing to be servants of the oligarchy. The internet, social media, and other evolving technologies enabled the message to spread its tentacles globally and instantaneously. The top echelon of the corporatocracy, the oligarchs, had become billionaires who had immense power over the media, politicians, and the judicial system. The idea of "one person, one vote" was no longer valid; it had become obvious that billionaires were positioned to buy elections.

As the corporatocracy expanded outward across the planet, something else happened—something that was clearly visible and at the same time ignored. Entire communities in the United States came to resemble the kinds of landscapes I had seen in the countries we'd exploited in Africa, Asia, Latin America, and the Middle East: dilapidated buildings, polluted rivers, crumbling infrastructure, towns stripped of opportunity, people deprived of hope.

Trump exploited the hopelessness and pain. He staged media events that highlighted the physical and social decay. He amplified the problems and then connected them to a vision of salvation anchored in his brand. He presented himself as a common man—not someone born with a silver spoon in his mouth, but someone who had managed to fight his way over gigantic obstacles into mythological success. His tactics included shocking large television audiences into believing that he was a decisive and rational executive by shaking his finger in people's faces and growling, "You're fired!" He often used the phrase "They're not coming after me. They're coming after you." After his June 2023 federal indictment, he told supporters at GOP events that his legal issues were persecution against his followers. Adhering to the script used by autocratic leaders in other countries, he presented himself as a hero standing in the way of those persecutions. He asserted that the investigations were efforts to stop the will of the American people, not just him personally.[9]

Like our fancy reports and sophisticated economic studies, the art of the story became Trump's most potent weapon. He was the savior, the infallible dealmaker, the master businessman (despite his bankruptcies), the outsider fighting corrupt politicians. Facts and figures mattered less than the fear he generated through stories of a betrayed America, corrupt insiders, and sinister outsiders. The message was unmistakable: *The world is a dangerous place. Fear it and turn to me. Only I can protect you.*

What do I consider to be the foundations of Trump's tactics? They are described in the third edition of *Confessions* as the four pillars of the EHM strategy.

THE FOUR PILLARS

The modern economic hit man system rests on four interlocking pillars, each reinforcing the others: fear, debt, anxiety over insufficiency (of food, housing, etc.), and divide and conquer. All are designed to consolidate wealth and power in the corporatocracy and its top brass, the oligarchy. For decades, these pillars were exported abroad, part of an arsenal that shaped the destinies of distant nations. But as the corporatocracy grew more entrenched and more global, its focus shifted inward. The United States became its richest resource.

Historically, the strategy leaned heavily on fear caused by military intimidation, and usually this led to the implementation of the other three pillars. For example: Ruler A defeated Ruler B in a war that devastated B's lands; A put B into debt by offering his daughter in marriage, investing in the restoration of B's lands, and promising to increase prosperity for B's impoverished people; and, as an important condition for such "generosity," A demanded that B would help A divide and conquer neighboring states.

Donald Trump entered politics precisely as these four pillars were reaching maturity on American soil. What once required covert strategies and clandestine financial manipulation could now be executed through mass media and hyper-partisan politics. It included legalizing what previously had been considered as corruption. Above all, it relied on the spectacle of personality. These four pillars have supported empire-building autocrats for centuries. However, in modern times their application is marching us into the minefield of a Death Economy.

Trump didn't invent the four pillars. But he stood atop them more visibly than any public figure in modern American history. To understand his significance—not as an anomaly but as an evolutionary milestone—we must explore how each pillar helped pave his path.

3

Pillar #1: Fear (First Term)

FEAR IS LEVERAGE. It has been the cornerstone of empire-builders throughout history. Today, fear convinces leaders to sign predatory loans and persuades nations to sell off resources. Fear binds populations to the very systems that exploit them. The fear of invasion, starvation, internal chaos, or of a country's own government drives people to accept dictatorial leadership. Fear is then exploited to justify the concentration of power, personal greed, and corruption. Autocrats demand loyalty in exchange for protection. Fear allows them to bully other countries into joining their imperial alliances, and to impose draconian measures on their own citizens. The pillar of fear supported the rise of fascist governments in Germany, Japan, Italy, and Spain that led to World War II. Today it is a key to the control exerted over their people by brutal autocrats in Russia, Iran, and North Korea.

Fear thus becomes the foundation of legitimacy, cloaked in the language of security and stability. Once the economic hit man system takes over, fear continues to sustain it through discipline, control, and threats of retribution. Subjects may obey not out of devotion but out of fears of retaliation. Propaganda and shows of force constantly remind the populace of the consequences of defiance.

The Cold War played a large role in instilling fear among US citizens and in foreign nations during my years on the job. Washington spread the belief that if the Communists defeated us in Vietnam, the rest of Southeast Asia would fall like dominoes. At the same time, the Soviet Union was, we were assured, using Cuba to spread the red tide of Communism throughout Latin America. The implication was that the Soviets and Chinese had their sights set on conquering Europe and the United States.

COMMUNISM AND OIL

My first assignment as an economic hit man took me to Indonesia. During meetings there, I frequently reminded President Suharto and other government and business leaders of the threat they faced from China, the Soviet Union, and the Communist regimes in Cambodia, Laos, and Vietnam. My message: Accept World Bank loans, collateralize them with Indonesian oil, and hire our companies to build massive infrastructure projects (making huge profits in the process), and we will protect you. We will also provide you with fancy reports you can use to justify your actions to your people.

I was highly successful. Indonesia signed onto the loans, US engineering and tech companies profited handsomely from projects they designed and helped build, and US oil companies (to paraphrase Trump) "drilled baby, drilled." I was soon promoted to Chief Economist and Director of Economic Development and Regional Planning.

Then came the oil embargo.

In the early 1970s, the Organization of Petroleum Exporting Countries (OPEC) imposed an embargo that threatened to hurl the United States into the depths of another Great Depression. Because OPEC was led by Saudi Arabia, that country was the key to ending the embargo and ensuring that it would never happen again.

The US Treasury Department hired MAIN to develop a strategy. I was designated as a team leader. But I had a problem.

The debt trap had worked in Indonesia because it was a poor country. However, Saudi Arabia enjoyed one of the world's highest per capita incomes and could not be enticed by loans.

What to do? The answer: Strike fear into the hearts of Saudi leaders.

It didn't take much to convince the Saudis that US ally Israel might attack at any moment. The Yom Kippur War that had pitted Egyptian and Syrian forces against Israel was fought in October 1973, several months before I arrived in Riyadh. The history of Western colonialism in the entire Middle East made Saudi Arabia well aware that it was vulnerable to foreign powers. In addition, the Royal House of Saud was terrified of attempts to overthrow or assassinate family members.

Saudi Arabia had a long history of coups and uprisings. Its monarch, King Faisal, had come to power in 1964 by deposing his brother, King Saud. In 1969, Faisal had arrested hundreds of military officers, including generals, for allegedly planning to overthrow him, and he suspected that the CIA had been a collaborator. During the 1960s and 1970s other governments were toppled in the Middle East, including the 1969 coup by Muammar Gaddafi that ended Libya's monarchy and sent a message throughout the region that kings could be replaced.

Thus, my job was to convince King Faisal and his family that they needed US protection (including from CIA jackals). The full story of how my colleagues and I accomplished this is described in detail in the third edition of *Confessions*. The nutshell version: We hammered out a deal that guaranteed US protection of the royal family—and the country itself—in exchange for its promise to stop any future attempts at OPEC embargoes, ensure that oil would always be sold for US dollars, invest Saudi petrodollars in US Treasury securities, and let the US Treasury Department apply the interest (which would total billions of dollars) from those securities to hire US firms to modernize (westernize) Saudi Arabia.

The two very different situations in Indonesia and Saudi Arabia proved to me that fear was a flexible and extremely effective tool for building an empire. Donald Trump was learning the same lessons and would employ fear very effectively as he built his own empire.

FROM REAL ESTATE TO POLITICS

Most US presidents have used fear to increase their own popularity and power. For example, Clinton struck fear of Al-Qaeda in American hearts after the 1998 bombings of US embassies in East Africa and was criticized for doing it to distract from the Monica Lewinsky scandal. Both Bushes invoked fear of Saddam Hussein to justify increasing their military powers. But Trump is the first in my memory to make fear central to his strategy for success, both in business and politics.

His economic hit man tactics began when he was a real estate developer.

In 1988, I walked into the tae kwon do dojang in Palm Beach County, Florida, where I practiced. A fellow black belt, a friend who owned a contracting business, was fiercely beating up on one of the heavy bags. He was striking at it as hard as he could with his hands and feet. He looked angry as hell.

"Hey Mike," I called out, thinking that if I ended up sparring with him, I would have to be very careful. "What's up?"

He stopped and glared at me. "I'm pretending this bag is that bastard Trump."

"What've you got against him?"

He stepped away from the bag. "I had a contract to install equipment worth $1 million at Mar-a-Lago. I did the job. When I presented the agreed-upon bill, I heard from one of his lawyers. 'We'll pay you $600,000,' he said. 'If you don't like it, take us to court. I assure you that your legal fees will exceed the $400,000 difference.'"

Since then, I've heard and read similar, well-documented stories about Trump cheating people through the fear of threats of legal action, character assassination, and financial ruin.[10]

Once he moved into politics, Trump campaigned by invoking these and a cornucopia of other fears: fear of immigrants, fear of losing jobs, fear of global competition, fear of cultural displacement, fear of decline, and fear of betrayal by the other political party. As economic hit men have always done, he promised that the antidote was dependency on him.

Trump's fear tactics during his first term were very different from those he employed in the first year of his second term. Consequently, I've divided this chapter into two sections. Since this distinction is not nearly as pronounced for the other three pillars, I've not made that distinction in the subsequent chapters.

THE FIRST FOUR YEARS

Trump's first term (2017–2021) was a master class in turning fear into leverage, and leverage into power. What follows are some of the most consequential examples, each demonstrating how fear became the central mechanism through which Trump consolidated influence, reshaped institutions, and deepened his control over the people he was elected to serve.

Trump's first major act was not a policy; it was a narrative.

His inaugural address—dark, foreboding, apocalyptic—painted the United States as a nation collapsing under crime, violence, corruption, and decay. He described America not as a world superpower but as a failed state, referring to "American carnage."

By inaugurating his presidency with a portrait of a country in ruin, Trump created emotional conditions that justified extraordinary executive power. He styled himself not just as president, but as savior. It echoed the psychological dynamic I'd seen in Ecuador, Chile, Guatemala, and Iran: First manufacture a sense of imminent collapse, then offer salvation on your terms.

FEAR OF FOREIGN ENEMIES

Early in his first term, Trump signed Executive Order 13769, which banned the citizens of seven Muslim-majority nations (Iraq, Syria, Iran, Libya, Somalia, Sudan, and Yemen) from entering the United States. Commonly referred to by critics and some of his own aides as the "Muslim ban," it carried a message of fear.[11]

The EHM strategy often begins by identifying an outside threat of foreigners. Forces beyond the borders must be contained. It was central to my work in many countries: In Indonesia, fear of China and other Communist Asian countries; in Iran, fear of the Soviet Union and Iraq; in Kuwait and Saudi Arabia, fear of Israel; in Egypt, fear of Israel and Libya. The list of the times and places where fear was used by economic hit men throughout history would fill the pages of a book.

Fear of the external "other" creates unity at home that is rooted not in shared hope but in divisive anxiety. In the 1970s United States, it was Communists. In Trump's 2017, it was Muslims.

The policy's legality was questionable. Its psychological intent was obvious: If the public believes there are invisible enemies flooding the borders, people will accept extraordinary measures to stop them.

But it did not stop with Muslims.

Trump described migrant caravans from Latin America as "invasions." He claimed criminals were pouring into the country unchecked. He portrayed the border as a war zone. The images—many misleading or taken out of context—achieved their goal: fear. And once fear reached a boiling point, Trump declared a national emergency to redirect military funds to build the border wall after Congress had refused to approve and fund it.[12]

The weaponization of the migrant "invasion" continued with the 2017–2018 "zero tolerance" directive that led to thousands of families being separated at the border. Trump openly stated that the purpose was deterrence. He weaponized trauma as policy, publicizing it to make others afraid. The message was effective not just for migrants, but for a domestic audience that came to see their president as someone willing to inflict cruelty to achieve his goals.

It was clear to me that his tactic was a page from the economic hit man handbook: Use partial truths to manufacture enemies, bypass democratic constraints, and consolidate power. It reminded me of the ways I had invoked fear of other countries, as well as internal Communists, to push foreign leaders into accepting World Bank loans. Trump touted fear of Muslims and migrants as justification for attempting to override the constitutional role of Congress.

THE DEEP STATE

While the foreign enemy narrative focused on migrants and Muslims, Trump deployed a parallel narrative at home: the idea of a "Deep State" conspiracy embedded within the FBI, CIA, Justice Department, and other institutions.[13]

When I worked abroad, one way to win over leaders like the shah of Iran and the emir of Kuwait was to convince them that their ministries and/or military were plotting against them and that we—the United States and our intelligence communities—could save them. Trump convinced his followers to fear US government agencies that had well-established reputations of combating both internal and external threats. He claimed that powerful institutions were plotting against him and, therefore, his supporters. Only he could save them. As reported by CNN on July 16, 2018:

> *US President Donald Trump, in a stunning rebuke of the US intelligence community, declined on Monday to endorse the US government's assessment that Russia interfered in the 2016 presidential*

election, saying he doesn't "see any reason why" Russia would be responsible.[14]

The effect was profound: This tactic eroded trust in the FBI, CIA, and the rest of the intelligence community; vilified career civil servants; and incited the public to fear their agencies. Loyalty to truth was replaced by loyalty to one person: the president. This allowed Trump to exert pressure on institutions that might otherwise check presidential power. In weakening institutions, he gained power.

Under Trump's leadership, a very different and very real Deep State emerged in the United States: the oligarchy. It consisted of a handful of extremely wealthy and powerful individuals who also had managed to gain extreme influence over Congress and the Supreme Court. Under Trump, the three branches of government, which were supposed to provide checks and balances to defend democracy, had all lined up to support a new oligarchy. Trump was a member, a symbol, and the new leader.

ATTACKING THE MEDIA

My training included lessons in economic hit man history. Two of the most important examples had happened in the early 1950s when the democratically elected prime minister of Iran (Mohammad Mosaddegh) and democratically elected president of Guatemala (Jacobo Árbenz) were overthrown in CIA-orchestrated coups. Preceding both coups were strong campaigns to discredit any media that supported these legitimately elected leaders. At the same time, US-funded media blitzes—in the two countries and the United States—portrayed each of them as an anti-democratic, pro-Soviet dictator. The reality was that their replacements (the shah in Iran and Castillo Armas in Guatemala) were in fact dictators.

Trump framed much of the US press as the "enemy of the people," borrowing a phrase used by the post-coup Iranian and

Guatemalan dictators and other authoritarian regimes since then. The tactic was familiar. Economic hit men thrive in environments where truth is destabilized and institutions cannot challenge the narrative. Trump popularized the term "fake news" and repeatedly used it to discredit legitimate information when it was at odds with his fabricated stories. Fear of misinformation—real or invented—creates distrust. And distrust concentrates power upward. You should trust the leader, not the journalists. You should trust the leader, not so-called independent investigators. You should trust the leader when you cannot trust facts.

There were exceptions: A few outlets (such as Fox, right-wing podcasts, and social media pundits) backed Trump, and he claimed that they—and only they—were objective. By destroying trust in those who criticized him, Trump became the single point of authority.

FEAR OF CHINA

During the two decades after the end of WWII, Washington portrayed China as a bulwark of the Communist march to world domination and a threat to US hegemony. This pillar of fear played a large role in justifying the continued exhaustion of resources, tax dollars, and American lives during the Vietnam War.

When I was on my first assignment in Indonesia in 1971, fear of China was one of my most effective tools. I used it to persuade the Suharto government to accept our loans and hire our companies to build infrastructure projects and implement anti-Communist programs.

However, beginning with President Nixon's 1972 trip to China, his administration and subsequent ones attempted to lower the tension. Before Trump's first term, President Obama had pursued a complex balance of cooperation on global issues while simultaneously engaging in trade competition with China as a vehicle for promoting US business in the Asia-Pacific region. This approach was central to his "Pivot to Asia" foreign policy strategy.

Trump reversed this and launched a vicious trade war with China that was framed not simply as an economic negotiation but as a clash of cultures. China was an enemy, not just a competitor.

More and more Americans saw China as a predatory force stealing American jobs and humiliating the United States on the global stage. The Chinese Communist Party (CCP) was portrayed as a strategic adversary and a threat to America's economic and political model. China became an example of the way I had used the specter of foreign rivals to persuade countries to side with the United States.

During Trump's first term, he used fear of China to justify sweeping tariff actions, unilateral executive moves, and a dramatic reshaping of global supply chains. The public was asked to absorb rising costs and market instability in the name of national defense. Trump understood that crisis creates obedience and obedience forfeits power to the person in charge.

SANCTIONS, TARIFFS, AND TERRORISTS

Trump's fear tactics took traditional economic hit man tactics to new levels with numerous threats of tariffs and sanctions against other countries. The fact that the tariffs were erratically imposed, unpredictably applied, often revised, and sometimes suspended created uncertainty around US policies. The uncertainty heightened fears about what the United States might do next.

In addition to China, Trump imposed sanctions at a record pace on many US trading partners. He nearly doubled the average annual amounts imposed by Presidents Obama and George W. Bush. Furthermore, Trump made extensive use of "maximum pressure" economic threats of sanctions aimed at severely damaging the economies of China, North Korea, Iran, and Venezuela. Ironically, these rarely translated into the behavioral changes they were designed to produce. Authoritarian governments passed the economic pain on to their populations rather than making strategic concessions. Pressure by a foreign government strengthened nationalist narratives that blamed US hostility for domestic hardship, which actually helped the targeted governments politically at home. Nevertheless, Trump touted them as successes.

Along with tariffs and sanctions, Trump invoked the threat of terrorism—both foreign and domestic—to increase his control over other countries and to expand executive authority. He frequently applied the "terrorist" label to domestic political opponents, such as antifa—even though many in law enforcement recognized antifa as a decentralized movement, not a formal organization.

Trump implemented an immense expansion of terrorist designations and presidential emergency powers during this presidential term. In one year alone, he listed twenty-four groups as foreign terrorist organizations, more than the total listed in the previous ten years combined. His interpretation of "terrorism" expanded way beyond definitions accepted by previous administrations. The financial backers of organizations designated as terrorist were vulnerable to sanctions.

He ordered the Pentagon to conduct a wide range of military activities and air strikes against so-called terrorist organizations, most notably in Somalia and Yemen. It was a tactic that increased the executive's latitude in deploying US military forces without explicit congressional approval for each operation. In retrospect, it laid the foundations for actions taken during his second term.

I was not surprised to hear lawyers describe Trump's tariffs, sanctions, and antiterrorist measures as targeting political opposition and exceeding constitutional boundaries.

THE PANDEMIC

COVID-19 presented a real crisis, not an invented one. A unifying president could have used the fears generated by that crisis to inspire his nation to come together. Instead, Trump used it to amplify a divisive panic. He alternated between (1) amplifying fear, referring to an "invisible enemy" and calling himself a "wartime president"; (2) deflecting fear onto China (the "kung flu," caused by a "China virus"); and (3) applying fear to discredit scientific studies and authorities, such as opposing and undermining the director of the National Institute of Allergy and Infectious diseases, Dr. Anthony Fauci.

By fragmenting the public's emotional response, Trump ensured that loyalty to him—not trust in science or institutions—became the determining factor in how millions of Americans understood the pandemic. In the process, he set the stage for a wide range of conspiracy theories around medicines, vaccines, climate change, and science in general.

He captured the fear response and redirected it inward. This is a hallmark of the EHM strategy: Fear becomes a tool not for solving crises but for tightening the leader's psychological hold over the population.

THE 2020–2021 PROTESTS AND INSURRECTION: FEAR OF INTERNAL CHAOS

When protests erupted in 2020 after the murder of George Floyd, Trump responded with a narrative of national collapse. He described cities as "war zones." He called protesters "terrorists," "anarchists," and "thugs." He deployed federal agents to Portland, Oregon, without local consent. Citizens there and elsewhere complained that this was not law enforcement; it was political theater.

The spectacle of heavily armed federal agents battling unarmed citizens served a purpose: to reinforce the image of Trump as the only force preventing total collapse. Just as economic hit men use military presence abroad to bolster their projects, Trump uses domestic paramilitary displays to consolidate his image as protector-in-chief.

The most consequential use of fear came at the end of Trump's first term. Months before the 2020 election, he began asserting that the vote would be fraudulent if he lost. He said mail-in ballots were corrupt. He claimed shadowy forces were stealing the country. He reframed a democratic process into an existential threat.

Economic hit men call this "preloading the narrative." If a deal is going to fail, you plant the belief that external forces sabotaged it. That way, your followers never lose faith. Trump applied this tactic to democracy itself. The fear he cultivated—of betrayal, of conspiracies, of stolen sovereignty—primed millions of Americans to reject his defeat in advance.

Their fears led to dependency on him as the savior. That dependency led to cultish loyalty. Loyalty led to January 6, 2021.

4

Pillar #1: Fear (Second Term)

IN MY ECONOMIC HIT MAN YEARS, we operated in the shadows. MAIN had a strict rule of not talking to the press, unless permission was granted by a senior vice president and used for strategic, transactional purposes. We whispered threats behind closed doors, dressed coercion in spreadsheets, and camouflaged domination as development. Our policy while dealing with the public was to remain mute. Subtle threats were enough to bend leaders to our will.

As Trump began his second term, all that had changed. The tactics I knew so well were tweeted, broadcast, livestreamed, and amplified. Fear was no longer a secret weapon—it was an out-in-the-open strategy.

THE SECOND INAUGURAL ADDRESS

Trump's 2017 inaugural address had painted a grim, fear-provoking portrait of economic decline, corruption, failing schools, drugs, and "rusted-out factories."

The address he delivered at his 2025 inauguration was very different. In a speech that was almost twice as long, he aimed to arouse specific, concrete fears that could only be relieved through executive orders and presidential commands. During that speech or subsequent ones, Trump declared a national emergency at the southern border. And another in the US energy sector, where he promised to loosen restrictions on drilling and fossil fuel production and return to heavy use of US oil and gas instead of wind and solar (as reflected in his "drill, baby, drill" slogan). He vilified "woke" ideas and diversity, equity, and inclusion (DEI) programs, describing them as threatening to destroy American culture and morals. He invoked fears of China. He called for "taking back" the Panama Canal, acquiring Greenland, and renaming the Gulf of Mexico the "Gulf of America" and the Department of Defense the Department of War.

There were two especially notable features in the speeches he gave in early 2025 that contrasted sharply with the 2017 address.

Trump declared his 2025 win a "mandate" because he won both the Electoral College and the popular vote, as opposed to 2017, when he lost the popular vote to Hillary Clinton by almost 2.9 million votes. However, by most standards it was far from a mandate. His popular vote margin in 2025 was one of the slimmest for a victorious candidate in US history. Furthermore, Republican majorities in the House and Senate were narrow, not the type of overwhelming control that supported his claims of a landslide. Nonetheless, he used his slim victory as a justification for the aggressive policy agendas he outlined elsewhere in the speech.

Perhaps even more significant, Trump's excessive use of first person heralded his narcissistic approach to governance. According to one analysis, he used "I" thirty-three times and "me/my" seventeen times in the 2025 speech, compared to just four times for both pronouns in the 2017 speech.[15] Judging by his language, Trump aimed to position himself not as a president of a democracy, but as an authoritarian leader whose personal grievances and ambitions would determine government actions.

"My recent election," he said during the 2025 inaugural address, "is a mandate to completely and totally reverse a horrible betrayal and all of these many betrayals that have taken place." This was a reference to his false claim that the 2020 election had been stolen from him, and to his four separate criminal indictments—most of them dismissed upon his election. It was also a scare tactic—a warning to anyone who might stand against him, including the media and members of his own party.

His speeches were those of one who rules, not governs. He would immediately start issuing executive orders and demanding personal loyalty and flattery, like a monarch. He surrounded himself with billionaires who groveled to receive his graces. He envisioned and decorated the White House in the image of a palace rather than a house of the people, including having the historic East Wing torn down and ordering its replacement with a massive ballroom, reminiscent of the gilded throne rooms of Russian czars and European kings. He was the "Peace President" who bombed seven countries, attacked fishing boats in the Caribbean, and started a war with Iran.

Trump's determination to turn his words into actions and establish his absolute authority was demonstrated most dramatically on January 3, 2026, when he sent a massive military force into Venezuela to capture the country's self-proclaimed president. Code-named Operation Absolute Resolve, it was not merely an attempt to overthrow a government. It was the ultimate act in an EHM strategy: When economic tactics fail, send in the jackals. It offered the world an extreme show of force like those taken in the past by monarchs and emperors obsessed with demonstrating their personal power. And it served as a warning to leaders around the world: Play the US's game or else . . .

Whether he saw himself as a monarch or not, Trump was acting as both an economic hit man and a jackal. While in my era we economic hit men were low-profile, the jackals acted out in the open. I offered a carrot; the jackals brandished the stick.

When the jackals did strike, their coups and assassinations were broadcast far and wide. US officials openly bragged about killing Libyan leader Muammar Gaddafi in 2011 and Iraqi leader Saddam Hussein in 2006. During Trump's first term, he ordered the drone killing of Iranian general Qasem Soleimani. The videos that were showcased had a chilling effect on the heads of state who might have considered opposing Trump's policies.

The only two of my clients who had rejected my offers—Ecuadorian President Jaime Roldós and Panamanian head of state Omar Torrijos—died in suspicious private plane crashes. Whether true or not, the possibility that these were assassinations caused fear among other countries' leaders who might be tempted to resist our deals. My meetings with them had been quiet; the plane crashes were horrifyingly public.

After this second inaugural address, I watched as Trump took on what to me was the persona of economic hit man and jackal combined. He was supported, like I had been, by a ready-made plan. Project 2025 enabled him to radically change the United States and its government virtually overnight.

PROJECT 2025

Project 2025 is a sweeping strategy for executing a conservative agenda. It was developed by the Heritage Foundation in April 2022. Among its proposals: dismantling government agencies, replacing top military brass and judges with people who fit the strategy's profiles, transforming civil service positions into political appointments, reducing or eliminating environmental protection regulations, curtailing agencies tied to DEI, vilifying media that criticize the president, gutting educational and research institutions, overhauling immigration and asylum laws, coercing elected officials from both parties to support the Project's agenda, and reducing oversight and balance-of-power mechanisms.[16]

Although discussions around Project 2025 have divided the United States between red and blue cities and states, conservatives and liberals, the Project has generated a common emotion: fear.

During the 2024 campaign Trump repeatedly distanced himself from Project 2025, claiming "I know nothing. . . . I have no idea who is behind it." But by late 2025, he openly embraced it. A post on his social media announced a meeting with Russ Vought, "of Project 2025 fame," to decide which federal agencies to cut and which to restructure.[17] That and other admissions exposed Project 2025 as the earthquake behind the tsunami of radical change that swept across America—and the world—during Trump's first year of his second term. The deluge of new policies, executive orders, pardons, laws, and lawsuits was so overwhelming that people grew numb to them. There seemed to be no way to stop the torrent of information and misinformation. Project 2025 had constructed a new EHM strategy.

The first year of Trump's second term, the 250th anniversary of the beginning of the American Revolution, ushered in what appeared to be an autocracy not unlike the one our founding fathers rebelled against. At the end of that year, I decided to write this book. My father was one of millions of Americans who fought in World War II to defend a republic that has inspired the world for those two and a half centuries and now is threatened by a rising oligarchy instigated by one man and enabled by an enfeebled Republican Party and a Supreme Court that seems intent on expanding executive power. What follows are some of the most blatant examples of how fear became the weapon of preference wielded by Trump to serve his and his family's interests—at the expense of those he was elected to serve.

ENVIRONMENTAL PROTECTIONS ROLLBACK

After leaving my job as an economic hit man, I spent the next decade studying and developing alternative energy projects. At first, the emphasis was on alleviating the acid rain produced by coal plants. But we soon discovered that the carbon dioxide produced by fossil fuels was an even greater problem. Over the ensuing years, entrepreneurs and scientists continued to make wind and solar more efficient and affordable. An optimistic pattern emerged that would position the United States as a leader in ridding the world of fossil fuels and their negative environmental impacts. Trump sought to reverse that pattern.

He raised fears with his baseless claims that solar, wind, and other forms of non–fossil fuel energy endangered US national security. People who protested gas pipelines, opposed drilling in ecologically sensitive regions, and promoted wind and solar technologies and electric cars were classified as dangerous impediments to progress.

On his first day back in office, Trump signed executive orders to promote resource extraction in Alaska and expedite drilling and energy exploitation—policies that mirror Project 2025's calls to dismantle or neuter major environmental and climate regulation efforts.

As the year progressed, he continued to hollow out and reverse the laws and regulations that protected fragile lands and communities. His administration's proposed massive budget cuts (over $1 billion) and staffing reductions at national parks caused closures to trails, visitor centers, and campgrounds; reduced services; and jeopardized operations at hundreds of park sites.[18]

I was reminded of the many times I and other economic hit men used the fear of US economic recessions to undermine Indigenous campaigns that opposed oil exploration in the Amazon rainforests of Colombia, Ecuador, and Peru. This has also been part of our strategy for justifying the defense of dictatorial regimes in Iran, Kuwait, Nigeria, Saudi Arabia, and other oil-rich countries.

My involvement in these activities had been a direct contradiction of my Peace Corps experiences. I had endured many a sleepless night fretting over it. In the end, it was one of the many factors that eventually convinced me to quit my job. Now I was watching the same activities being implemented on a national level and across the planet.

ELIMINATION OF DEI IN FEDERAL AGENCIES

Trump exploited the fears of white people, especially white men, that their jobs and way of life were threatened by the DEI policies of former administrations. He claimed that such programs lead to "reverse discrimination" against white men, undermine merit-based achievement, and constitute "political indoctrination."

Early in his second term, Trump signed Executive Order 14151, titled "Ending Radical and Wasteful Government DEI Programs and Preferencing," which effectively terminated DEI programs and roles across federal departments.

This order mirrored Project 2025's broader goal of removing DEI initiatives from government agencies—a move that worries civil rights advocates and many in marginalized communities, who fear that systemic protections and inclusion efforts could erode.

I learned early in my economic hit man career to exploit cultural, religious, and racial differences in ways that incited fear. This was particularly true in areas with a history of tribalism and colonialism, including many Middle Eastern, African, and Latin American countries that had oil and other resources the United States coveted. For example, oil company economic hit men threatened and bribed local Indigenous leaders in the regions of Ecuador, where I'd been a Peace Corps volunteer, into persuading their people to accept oil drilling projects. They pitted communities against each other. When leaders who resisted were found dead, the economic hit men blamed the "terrorists" from another community. Ultimately, these projects poured millions of gallons of toxic waste into the water supply systems, causing severe environmental damage and health problems.

CIVIL SERVICE PURGE

Trump raised fears that professional, nonpartisan civil servants constituted a "Deep State" or were "rogue bureaucrats" who undermined democracy and were disloyal, incompetent, or simply more interested in keeping their jobs than implementing the president's agenda. The reality is that many of those civil servants were actually educated experts in their fields and are not easily replaced. Although Trump did not invent them, he capitalized on existing conspiracy theories—such as QAnon, "Spygate," election fraud, and the justification of the January 6 riots as legitimate—to animate his base.

It was a throwback to strategies I implemented when the IMF offered to restructure loans to countries that could not pay their World Bank debts. In exchange for the new deals, we demanded that the countries accept Structural Adjustment Programs (SAPs), which often required imposing massive layoffs, lowering taxes on the rich and wages for the average worker, and replacing government workers who objected to such policies. In addition, these tactics were used as retribution against people appointed by previous administrations.

For Trump, it was a manifestation of the Project 2025 proposal to turn many civil service jobs into political appointments that gave the president far greater control over the bureaucracy. He replaced meritocracy with something more corrosive and dangerous: rule by the very rich, including the wealthiest cabinet in history and the idea that immense wealth is the single best qualification to govern a country.[19] "If you're so damn smart, why aren't you rich?"

In practice, the Trump administration used staffing moves, executive orders, and budget pressures to reshape the administrative state and undermine institutional continuity, expertise, and the nonpartisan civil service that (in theory) acts as a check against political whims.

IMMIGRATION ENFORCEMENT

Economic hit men throughout history have invoked fear of the "other" as a means for bolstering their policies. Trump cited national security, public safety (crime), and economic fears to justify his crackdown on immigrants. He repeatedly asserted that people entering the United States without legal permission were "criminals," "murderers," "rapists," and "drug lords." He alleged that other countries, including Venezuela and the Democratic Republic of Congo, were sending people from their prisons and mental institutions to the United States, posing a direct security threat. No proof of such generalized accusations was offered—just a few specific incidents, such as a shooting involving an Afghan national, to justify broad crackdowns.

Because migrants were presented as a top national security threat, Trump claimed that a strong vetting system was necessary to keep the country safe. This included targeting nationals from specific countries (often in the Middle East and Africa) with travel bans or increased scrutiny, claiming they are "noncompatible with Western civilization." The administration also suggested, without evidence, that transnational gangs and cartels (e.g., Tren de Aragua) were "invading" forces, and that countering the invasion required expanded executive powers.

Immigration and Customs Enforcement (ICE)—often masked, heavily armed, and showing no identification—had rounded up and detained more than seventy thousand migrants as of mid-January 2026, reaching record highs, with nearly 75 percent lacking any criminal record.[20] These resulted in mass deportation efforts and strained detention capacities. They struck fear into anyone, US citizen or otherwise, who might appear to be an "immigrant."

PANAMA

NBC News reported on March 13, 2025:

> *The White House has directed the U.S. military to draw up options to increase the American troop presence in Panama to achieve President Donald Trump's goal of "reclaiming" the Panama Canal, according to two U.S. officials familiar with the planning.*
>
> *In his joint address to Congress last week, Trump said that "to further enhance our national security, my administration will be reclaiming the Panama Canal."*[21]

That address to Congress set US–Latin American relations back decades. It brought up memories for me of the 1970s, when I was trying to negotiate deals with Panama's head of state, Omar Torrijos.

On my first trip, in 1972, I landed at Panama's Tocumen International Airport late one night during a tropical deluge. While riding to my hotel in a taxi, I stared out through windshield wipers at a billboard portrait of a handsome man with a prominent brow and flashing eyes. One side of his wide-brimmed hat was hooked rakishly up. I recognized him as the hero of modern Panama, Omar Torrijos.

I knew that Torrijos was extremely popular among his people because he was a firm defender of Panama's right to self-rule, its claims of sovereignty over the Panama Canal, and his demands that the United States remove its School of the Americas from the Canal Zone. This "school" was infamous for its role in training brutal right-wing generals and dictators—including notoriously ruthless ones from Argentina, Bolivia, Chile, El Salvador, Guatemala, and Haiti.

Panamanians wanted to end what they referred to as "Yankee colonialism" in the Canal Zone, a 553-square-mile swath of territory that bisected their country. The Zone was populated by stately buildings constructed in Renaissance European and Spanish

Colonial architectural styles, contrasting sharply with the poor Panamanian neighborhoods that sprawled outside the barbed-wire and chain-link fences protecting it. During that first visit, a government official, Fidel, drove me into the Zone. Fidel could only gain entry because he was accompanying me and I held a US passport.

"Everything in here is US property," Fidel explained. "All the businesses—the supermarkets, barbershops, beauty salons, restaurants, all of them—are exempt from Panamanian laws and taxes. There are seven 18-hole golf courses, US post offices scattered conveniently around, US courts of law and schools. It truly is a country within a country."

In the United States, there were many who hated Torrijos for the same reasons Panamanians loved him. They were determined to keep the Canal, the Zone, and the School of the Americas. Some went so far as to call for the United States to claim Panama as a US territory, like Puerto Rico and the Virgin Islands.

The animosity between Panama and those factions in the United States explained the caption beneath Torrijos's face on the billboard: "Omar's ideal is freedom; the missile is not invented that can kill an ideal!" A shiver ran down my spine as I sat in that taxi and read those words.

Several years later, during the 1976 presidential campaign, candidate Jimmy Carter promised to negotiate a treaty that would turn ownership of the Canal and Zone over to Panama. Carter won the election and fulfilled his campaign promise by negotiating and signing what were known as the Torrijos–Carter Treaties.

On the other hand, when Ronald Reagan defeated Carter in 1980, he threatened Panama with often-repeated variations of the phrase "We bought the Canal, we paid for it, it's ours, and we're going to keep it." He despised Torrijos, whom he referred to as "that tinhorn dictator."

Soon after Reagan took office in 1981, the Air Force plane carrying Torrijos crashed, killing him, the two pilots, a mechanic, and two of his bodyguards. Many in Panama and throughout Latin America accused Reagan of ordering Torrijos's assassination. Although there was never proof that it was anything but an accident, the suspicion sent shock waves of fear to leaders around the world who might have considered opposing the United States.

Similar fears struck Latin America after Trump's March 2025 address to Congress, and later his orders to send a large US Navy fleet to the Caribbean and off the shores of Panama. Insurance markets, investors, the tourist industry, and many other businesses were sent into turmoil. Trump didn't need to storm the Canal or Panama; he just needed the world to fear that he might. The shiver that had run down my spine when I saw that billboard rippled across the entire hemisphere.

Of course, the threat did not stop at Panama's borders. Leaders in many countries were scared into believing that Trump would go to any extreme to enforce his will.

CANADA, GREENLAND, AND NATO

Trump took the Panama threats to another level when he announced his ambitions to make Canada the fifty-first state and acquire Greenland. At first it seemed like it had to be a joke. Then his threats began to materialize through tariffs, cross-border trade disruptions, and supply chain choke points.

Canada, one of America's closest partners, suddenly found itself being treated like an enemy. Every decision that involved trade with the United States became a risk calculation. Every government choice carried the unspoken question: Will Washington retaliate? Behind the bluster was a scary message that echoed the Panama one: Your sovereignty is fragile.

Then came Greenland. During the January 2026 World Economic Forum in Davos, Trump threatened to annex Greenland and asked his military advisors for options to seize it. Europeans saw this as an effort to blow up NATO.

Greenland sits at the doorway to the Arctic, a region rich in minerals, rare earths, and future trade routes. Trump's threats alerted Russia and China to start positioning themselves for a major conflict. Since Greenland is an autonomous territory within the Kingdom of Denmark and Denmark is a member of NATO, European countries worried that they would be called on to defend Greenland, possibly doing the previously unthinkable: waging war against the United States. Panic reverberated through the corridors of NATO headquarters. Member countries immediately revved up their negotiations for trade deals and other alliances with China. An organization created out of fear of Russia now also feared America.

These were unprecedented policies, innuendos, and threats that generated uncertainty and fear—the jackal side of a US president.

Ironically, although Trump seemed determined to make tough guy Reagan look like a pussy cat, his policies strengthened Russia and China.

MILITARIZATION

Trump's demand that the Department of Defense change its name to the Department of War sent a shudder through America and the global community. It was a proclamation that all branches of the US military, including the National Guard and every person who works in the defense industry, are there to wage war, not to defend the nation. It is the military equivalent of "Shoot first, ask later."

The fear-mongering abductions by masked, armed, and hooded ICE agents are reminiscent of fascist regimes. This is not just an innocent change in policy, not merely about a government agency conducting raids that are probably illegal; it is also psychological warfare waged on US soil, often against US citizens. It is PSYOPs at its most basic, sadistic level.

Trump capped 2025 by sending a massive flotilla of destroyers, cruisers, submarines, amphibious assault ships, and the USS *Gerald*

R. Ford, the world's largest aircraft carrier and the largest warship ever built, into the Caribbean. Along with the ships, he deployed supporting aircraft and around fifteen thousand troops. Using drones, the military immediately began sinking boats they claimed were narcotraffickers and killing the people on board, who had not been charged with or found guilty of any crimes. In my day this would have been called "battleship diplomacy," which in actuality is not diplomacy at all.

Friends of mine in Latin America asked questions that went beyond the queries of whether or not the killings were legal: If you suspect Caribbean fishermen of working for a narco-kingpin, why would you kill them? Wouldn't you want to capture them, convince them to identify who they work for, and then apprehend the bosses? And why would you even consider granting a presidential pardon to a man like Juan Orlando Hernández, a former Honduran president who was serving a forty-five-year sentence in the United States for cocaine importation and related weapons offenses and was (according to the US Justice Department) "at the center of one of the largest and most violent drug trafficking conspiracies in the world?"[22] Who does that, my friends in Latin America wondered, except someone who benefits from the drug trade?

Having seen firsthand the militarization of countries in Latin America and the Middle East, I can say that Trump's actions in Minneapolis, Venezuela, Iran, and the Caribbean, and toward Greenland and Canada, resemble those of military dictatorships I witnessed in the past. They usually set the stage one city or event at a time. Trump demonstrated in Minneapolis that he has his own private militia—and in those other countries a military command—that is willing to execute acts just because he says they are legal, despite the fact that many legal scholars vehemently disagree.

These unprecedented, draconian shows of force terrorize people throughout the hemisphere and rekindle memories of the hated Monroe Doctrine and other US colonialist policies. Grabbing people off the street and blowing up fishing boats may have made

Trump look strong in the eyes of his MAGA followers, but such actions cause irreparable harm to the image of the United States as a defender of democracy and the rule of law. And those actions played into the hands of China's and Russia's economic hit men, who love nothing more than to exploit distrust in and anger at the United States.

I'm glad no US president implemented anything remotely approaching these self-destructive policies during my career. It would have made my job impossible.

2025 NATIONAL SECURITY STRATEGY

Trump issued his annual 2025 National Security Strategy (NSS) on December 5. It seemed a fitting way to bring the first year of his second term to closure. Its language was fear-laden, describing a "world on fire," the threat of internal domestic enemies, "uncontrolled" migration, ideological subversives, and betrayal by allies. In many ways it justified greater personal and presidential power, especially over law enforcement, security agencies, Congress, courts, foreign policy, and dissenting citizens.

The message was out in the open once again: Trump is the savior who must have absolute power to act quickly and decisively in the name of security. Forget about checks and balances. It was a call for dropping any pretense of democracy.

Portraying the Western Hemisphere as under siege, the NSS introduced a "Trump Corollary" to the Monroe Doctrine, asserting the president's right to act as a regional police power and intervene—including by using military force—against drug cartels, gangs, and other threats. It sent a clear warning to Latin America that the United States would not tolerate "hostile foreign incursion or ownership of key assets" by adversaries like China.

Although the NSS did not name Putin, it did identify Russia as a "revisionist power" and a threat. However, in the speech when Trump officially presented the document, he boasted that during a recent phone call with the Russian president, Putin had thanked the United States for a CIA tip that helped foil a terrorist attack in St. Petersburg. It was, Trump said, an example of cooperation between the two countries. That speech increased fears in Ukraine and among NATO countries that Trump would continue to encourage Putin's narcissism and Russia's aggression toward the rest of Europe.

When I read the NSS and commentaries about it, I felt like I was witnessing a return to the proclamations of authoritarian regimes that led to World Wars I and II. This fear was reinforced by the knowledge that the document must already have been drafted when, on November 30, 2025, Trump wrote on his Truth Social platform that Democratic lawmakers were guilty of seditious acts that were "punishable by DEATH!" It was his response to a video released by six Democratic members of Congress, all military or intelligence service veterans, reminding active service members that they have the right—in fact, the obligation—to refuse to obey illegal orders issued by their superiors.[23]

When a president casually suggests executing members of Congress or military officers who defy illegal orders, democracy is severely threatened. You don't need purges. You don't need trials. You only need people to imagine them. Self-censorship does the rest. Fear polishes the knives of repression.

The NSS has become the whetstone to sharpen those knives.

And the list goes on. Other tactics Trump has used that cause fear among many US residents and/or embolden his supporters and administration to act illegally or unethically include:

- National Guard deployments that became political theater and spread fear in American cities.
- Massive pardons—including for the January 6 perpetrators who threatened the lives of elected members of Congress and police officers; fraudsters like David Gentile, who was convicted of swindling thousands of people out of almost

$2 billion dollars; and convicted drug lord Juan Hernández—sending a message that "crime pays" as long as it is approved by Trump.

- Calls for gerrymandering to give Republicans more congressional seats and endanger the electoral process.
- Suspension of air defense weapons and rockets to Ukraine as an offering to Putin, a rejection of Biden policies, and a fear tactic to enforce a peace deal that he desperately hoped would net him a Nobel Peace Prize.
- Closures of Voice of America and the US Agency for International Development (USAID) to appease both Putin and Xi and send intimidating messages to other agencies and media outlets.
- The gift of massive tax breaks to billionaires through his One Big Beautiful Bill while increasing taxes on lower-income Americans who fear for the health of their families and the survival of ill and elderly members.
- Temporarily freezing federal funds to childcare facilities and thereby creating immense problems for parents who have nowhere to leave their children while they're at work.
- The termination of US participation in the Paris Agreement and COP30 in response to pressure and campaign donations from the fossil fuel industry, highlighting fears of more climate change–induced hardships and catastrophes.
- A habit of attacking those who question him in an attempt to intimidate them or undermine their credibility (such as telling CBS's Nancy Cordes, "You're just asking questions because you're a stupid person"; describing *New York Times* correspondent Katie Rogers as "third rate . . . ugly, both inside and out"; shouting at Bloomberg White House correspondent Catherine Lucey, "Quiet. Quiet, piggy"; and referring to immigrants as "garbage," "lowlifes," and similar).

- A pattern of using the presidency to line his own pockets and those of his family with millions of dollars through alleged deals cut with client countries, digital coin scams, insider trading, and other cons, and causing fears that the very foundations of a presidency for the people have collapsed. Reuters calculates that the Trump Organization's income for the first half of 2024 was about $51 million and about $864 million in the first half of 2025, a leap of roughly 1,600 percent. For comparison, Nvidia's net income increase was about 44 percent, which was considered exceptionally high.[24]

The economic hit man's pillar #1 (fear) has evolved and been digitized, weaponized, and turned inward. No more quiet threats in presidential palaces. No more secret deals behind mahogany doors. Fear now travels at the speed of a headline. The empire doesn't hide its tools. It broadcasts them. And the world—foreign and domestic—reacts exactly as the designers intended. Fear governs. Fear silences. Fear extracts.

In late 2024, I accepted an invitation to speak at a conference in the Republic of Georgia. Walking through the streets of Tbilisi, I thought about the years when this country was part of the Soviet Union. The very tools I'd once employed to fight Communist oligarchs Trump now was using on allies, rivals, and citizens of my own country. A new US oligarchy is attempting to tear down democracy. It is led by one man, who is also its spokesperson. The empire hasn't collapsed. It has metastasized. And every region of the planet is living inside its shadow.

Trump's first year of his second term was a volcanic eruption that sent a lava flow of promises, intimidations, executive orders, insults, corruption, and lies across the planet. He scuttled laws and well-established norms of decency that have defined America since its beginning. During one chaotic year, he managed to bury—at least temporarily—the world's oldest, most enduring attempt at democracy under an EHM strategy that I had once used to exploit other countries.

5

Pillar #2: Debt

The modern version of the EHM strategy can be summarized as follows.

A higher-income nation identifies lower-income nations that possess oil or other resources but lack sufficient means and/or the political will to develop them. The higher-income nation sends its EHMs to convince the lower-income nations to accept large loans. . . . An important condition is that the money is earmarked to hire higher-income-nation companies. . . . These companies reap huge profits and everyone else suffers because funds are diverted . . . to pay interest on the loans. . . . The debts are so large they can't be repaid. . . . This process is sometimes referred to as debt-trap diplomacy.

—*CONFESSIONS OF AN ECONOMIC HIT MAN*,
THIRD EDITION (PAGES 2–3)

I SPENT MANY HOURS inside rooms where we built empires on debt. We stacked loan packages so high that no nation could ever climb out. We sold the idea of prosperity, knowing we were engineering dependence. Nations don't have a monopoly on this model. Banks, corporations, and intelligence agencies run debt-trap operations too. And so do individuals. Trump is an extremely proficient debt-trapper.

To the traditional approach around saddling people with loans they can't pay, Trump adds one more weapon I never owned: the psychology of personal loyalty debt.

In the movie *The Godfather*, Vito Corleone tells the undertaker Bonasera, "You never even tried to be my friend. And you feared to be in my debt." Later he admitted, "I don't do favors, I accrue debts," and said that he used favors to create powerful, lasting obligations. Every culture I know has stories about kings and other autocrats who award favors to people with the goal of indebting them so they will be obligated to return the favor later, or else . . .

Trump—businessman, celebrity, political strongman—has turned debt into a personal and national operating system. It is not the kind that appears on balance sheets alone; it is also the kind that infiltrates relationships, governments, and institutions. Debt, monetary or personal, has been one of Trump's most reliable tools.

This chapter reveals how he adapted the economic hit man pillar #2 (debt) not to nations alone, but also to people, systems, and entire political structures.

MONETARY DEBT

From my first job in Indonesia to the last ones in Colombia and Panama, financial debt was my crowbar: Pry a country open with World Bank loans, slide in the corporations, and extract everything of value.

Trump mastered Plan B to this approach. He built a persona on lies about his business acumen; however, the real engine beneath his empire was debt—massive, chaotic, leverage-heavy debt that, in an odd twist to the story, made his creditors dependent on him. The banks he worked with were not clients; they were captives. Once they loaned him enough, they couldn't let him fail. Their debt became his weapon.

This was a classic economic hit man inversion: In traditional debt-trap diplomacy, lenders control borrowers. In Trump's debt-trap system, the borrower gains power over the lender. We had an agency to stop countries from doing what Trump does: the IMF. It would "offer" to refinance the loans if a country agreed to sell its resources cheaply to our corporations, allow the United States to build a military base on its soil, or make other concessions that served our purposes. I enclosed "offer" in quotation marks because it was not really an offer; it was a demand backed by the full weight of the US government and the international financial community. If the country refused to accept the IMF deal, rating agencies would downgrade it to the equivalent of an F, it would become a pariah, and it would likely be plagued by domestic turmoil, coups, or assassinations. We made it clear that jackals were waiting in the shadows.

But Trump's banks did not have either an IMF or a stable of jackals behind them. When the loans reached a certain level, the banks couldn't walk away. Trump was "too big to fail." The banks had to refinance and renegotiate the obligations. They became hooked on the hope of repayment.

An example is Trump's relationship with Deutsche Bank. After most major US banks refused to extend him large credits, Deutsche stepped in repeatedly to extend loans that at times totaled hundreds of millions and, by some accounts, over a billion dollars across multiple deals. Deutsche continued to finance deals even as red flags piled up, and in several later disputes the bank found itself negotiating with a debtor who could—and would—sue or litigate instead of paying. The bank refinanced and restructured rather than foreclosing, because cutting Trump loose risked large write-downs and reputational reverberations.[25]

Such tactics produced a reversal of the usual debt dynamic: Instead of a creditor holding all the leverage, the borrower's size and publicity made lenders reluctant to pull the plug. Banks that were supposed to enforce discipline became partners in keeping Trump afloat—and, in that role, vulnerable to pressure, lawsuits, and public controversy. The consequence is obvious in economic hit man terms: Create a mutual exposure so the counterparty will avoid collapse at all costs.

Trump wasn't just selling prosperity. He was selling avoidance of disaster for the banks and their officers.

FUDGED NUMBERS

I usually had to convince a country's leaders that the loans would drive future economic growth to high levels. I called on my staff of econometricians and computer modelers to produce reports that did exactly that. For example, we would show that if a country took out a loan and invested it by hiring US corporations to build an electric power system where none had previously existed, energy demand would increase at, say, 15 percent a year for twenty-five years. And that would boost economic growth by 7 percent a year. We always had those numbers in mind before we even began our studies. We knew the outcome we wanted. Here's an example from *The New Confessions of an Economic Hit Man* (lightly edited for brevity; pages 36–37):

> *Our team was quartered in the country's fanciest hotel, the Hotel InterContinental Indonesia. On the evening of our first day, our project manager, Charlie Illingworth, hosted a dinner for us in the elegant restaurant on the top floor.*
>
> *Charlie was a connoisseur of war; he devoted most of his free time to reading history books about great military leaders and battles. As usual, this night he was wearing khaki slacks and a short-sleeved khaki shirt with military-style epaulets.*
>
> *After welcoming us, he lit up a cigar. "To the good life," he sighed, raising a glass of champagne. We joined him. Our glasses clinked.*
>
> *Cigar smoke swirling around him, Charlie glanced about the room. "We're here to develop a master plan for the electrification of*

Java—the most populated land in the world. But that's just the tip of the iceberg."

His expression turned serious; he reminded me of George C. Scott playing General Patton, one of Charlie's heroes. "We are here to accomplish nothing short of saving this country from the clutches of Communism. As you know, Indonesia has a long and tragic history. Now, at a time when it is poised to launch itself into the twentieth century, it is tested once again. Our responsibility is to make sure that Indonesia doesn't follow in the footsteps of its northern neighbors, Vietnam, Cambodia, and Laos. An integrated electrical system is a key element. That, more than any other single factor, will ensure that capitalism and democracy rule."

He took another puff on his cigar and flipped past a couple of his note cards. "We all know how dependent our own country is on oil. Indonesia can be a powerful ally to us in that regard. So, as you develop this master plan, please do everything you can to make sure that the oil industry and all the others that serve it—ports, pipelines, construction companies—get whatever they are likely to need in the way of electricity for the entire duration of this twenty-five-year plan."

He raised his eyes from his note cards and looked directly at me. "Better to err on the high side than to underestimate. You don't want the blood of Indonesian children—or our own—on your hands. You don't want them to live under the hammer and sickle or the red flag of China!" Later, he let me know that he expected me to show electric load growth that averaged at least the unprecedented annual rate of 17 percent.

Trump's real estate empire depended not only on loans but on the constant creation of fudged accounting numbers that reassured partners while concealing fragility. Investigations, including an IRS audit uncovered by *ProPublica* and *The New York Times*, reveal aggressive tax and accounting claims that could materially affect Trump's obligations on high-profile projects. These maneuvers created an appearance of solvency that encouraged Trump to negotiate from the deceptive position of a winner even when cash flows were weak, and thereby enabled him to extract concession after concession from lenders and municipal partners.[26]

In short, Trump's tactics mirrored ones I'd used: Manufacture numbers that predict growth and present them in fancy reports to secure loans; then, when the loans collapse, renegotiate using your collateral as leverage (for me, a country's resources; for Trump, the pulpit of publicity and the threat of exposing the banks). That cycle transforms fudged numbers to leverage.

LOYALTY FAVORS

Money isn't the only currency that traps. Some debts can't be measured in dollars.

When I was sent to Iran and Saudi Arabia, I knew that I would never convince their governments to accept loans they couldn't repay. Their coffers overflowed with petrodollars. The way to win them over was to convince them that they needed US protection against the Soviet Union, neighboring countries, and internal enemies. We were, I said, the ones who had the intelligence services and military might to defend them, and we could build them electrical power grids, ports, airports, highways, and other infrastructure that would demonstrate to their people that they were the leaders who would catapult the nation into the modern world. Those improvements would keep their political enemies at bay. All they had to do was maintain their loyalty to us.

I didn't just say, "We will build you this infrastructure in exchange for your oil." I let them know that we were doing them a big favor and would expect them to return that favor by helping us control OPEC, build a military base in their country, or provide something else we needed from them.

Trump had learned this approach from his father and his mentor, the lawyer and fixer Roy Cohn. He'd also grown up and cut his teeth in Don Corleone's New York City, where he learned to create IOUs of loyalty the same way I once had. Whether spoken out loud or merely implied, the oath of loyalty is based on the debt of personal favors. "I made you," or "I protected you," or "I rescued you." In any case, "I can destroy you, if you don't . . ."

These psychological debts are as binding as mortgages.

Cabinet members, political operatives, congressional loyalists, lobbyists, and foreign leaders are drafted by Trump into a system of favor-based obligations. A pardon, a public defense, a campaign endorsement, a withheld attack or firing—they are all collateral. Those who accept the favor become assets. Those who refuse become targets.

Trump's inner circle operates less like a traditional political apparatus and more like a network of indebted clients or mobsters indebted to the Godfather. Each individual owes him something: access, reputation, survival. And each knows that default brings retaliation.[27]

This is classic economic hit man discipline. Its mantra: Never let a client forget the loyalty debt. Never let a client think the debt has been paid. Never stop hinting at what repayment might look like. Or what happens if repayment is not delivered. There is one caveat: The creditor, Trump, does not have to return that loyalty. He abandoned his former fixer, Michael Cohen, who served time in prison for crimes committed while in the employ of Donald Trump. He does not hesitate to fire those who have served him.

TRANSACTIONAL DEBTS

In the late 1970s, I spent time in Argentina with retired army general Charles Noble, a MAIN senior vice president who would soon become president. Chuck was a West Point graduate with a master's degree in engineering from MIT. He'd enjoyed a distinguished military career, having served as commanding general of the US Army Engineer Command in Vietnam.

Now he had traded his uniform for conservative dark suits, but he continued to crop his hair military short. He reflected his West Point training in almost every way, except for one: He sported black engineer's boots, like the ones favored by members of the Hells Angels. Sometimes the boots were spit-polished, but usually they were smudged with mud. They baffled me at first; they seemed totally out of character. After I got to know Chuck better, I realized that they were his way of setting himself apart; he was not a typical general, he was also a blood-and-guts engineer.

Argentina was ruled by a military dictatorship and was a founding member of Operation Condor, a covert campaign of state terror by South American dictatorships from 1975 to 1983. Its goal was to stop what the United States called the Red Tide of Communism. Buenos Aires was the command center of the operation's intelligence sharing, kidnappings, torture, and assassinations of political opponents across international borders. The infamous Automotores Orletti clandestine detention center there was a main hub for imprisoning and torturing victims from various countries.

One of the ways the United States supported Operation Condor was to provide loans used to build infrastructure projects. Officially, Chuck was in Argentina as MAIN's project manager of the massive Salto Grande hydroelectric project. Unofficially, Chuck and I were there to make sure that Argentina honored its commitments of working closely with Washington in the drive to stop global Communism.

One of my jobs was to offer "transactional debts." I particularly recall sitting in a private dining room in one of Argentina's most elegant and exclusive restaurants, along with half a dozen men who were top aides to the leader of Argentina's dictatorship, General Jorge Rafael Videla.

After a dinner of Argentine steak and wine, we sat beneath an ornate crystal chandelier, sipping vintage cognac and smoking Cuban cigars—all of it on MAIN's bill, of course. A beautiful woman in a flamenco dress sat in a corner strumming a guitar. The scent of her perfume mingled with that of the cigar smoke that swirled up and around the chandelier.

I tapped my glass. The room went silent. "I'm happy to announce," I said, "that MAIN has agreed to guarantee your sons and daughters acceptance at one of Boston's elite colleges. We will grant them full scholarships, all expenses paid. We'll also offer them jobs when they graduate if they choose to work for us." It was a bribe, pure and simple—and totally legal under both US and Argentine law. When accepted, it was transformed into a transactional debt.

During that same trip, I negotiated other similar transactions. Behind closed doors, I committed our company to overpaying construction subcontractors, as well as vendors who provided food and other goods and services to our employees. Of course, those businesses were owned by family members of top government officials. The implication was that the excess profits would be shared by the government officials. These were outright bribes hidden in the dark cloak of legality. If ever questioned by any authority, they could be justified simply as bad business decisions.

Trump doesn't treat power merely as authority. He also treats it as a transactional commodity. Everything is negotiable, and the currency of trade includes regulatory intervention, political endorsements, legal protection, ambassadorships, and policy commitments. Each becomes a chip in a transactional debt economy—issued, traded, and collected. He gives something valuable. He expects repayment in services. If repayment falters, he raises the price. If it collapses, he forecloses, with public shaming, political destruction, or legal threats.

It is predatory lending applied to human relationships.

If we overlay the economic hit man sequence onto Trump's tactics, the structure becomes obvious. It is a replay of the strategy I used in Argentina:

1. *Identify a vulnerability*: a business failure, a politician under pressure, a regulator seeking a service, a foreign leader needing access, a voter dissatisfied by the status quo.

2. *Create dependence*: through funding, endorsements, or protection; by offering legitimacy or access to "fixers," mailing lists, networks, and information.
3. *Establish the debt*: "You wouldn't be here without me," "you can't do it without me," and "you owe me."
4. *Extract repayment*: through loyalty, silence, endorsements, policy changes, votes, or compliance.
5. *Enforce consequences if a default*: through boycotts, sanctions, mockery, legal pressure ("taking me to court will ruin you"), public humiliation, or political exile.

This is not politics. It is not business as usual. It is a tactic in pillar #2 of the economic hit man game: a system of individualized, weaponized transactions.

DEBT AS COERCION

Once we economic hit men had sunk a country over its head with debt, we could demand that it transfer its collateral of oil, minerals, labor, or other assets to our corporations. Through IMF Structural Adjustment Programs (SAPs), we had the power to coerce the country into submission.

Trump's casino deals are textbook cases of debt used as a tool of coercion rather than mere financing. The Trump Taj Mahal in Atlantic City, financed with high-interest junk bonds, collapsed into bankruptcy after the 1990s downturn. Rather than exit, Trump repeatedly negotiated restructurings that left him with control even as ownership and obligations shifted to bondholders. Four casino-related bankruptcies taught the same lesson: Leverage down creditors, restructure ownership, hold on to the brand and public image, and use the sheer scale of interconnected claims to prevent creditors from "calling the shots."[28]

That was a basic economic hit man maneuver recast for a private firm: Leverage collateral as vehicles of exploitation. In this case, the collateral was reputation and the value of the Trump name, a brand that kept markets and backers invested even after repeated defaults.

Trump's power to make or break politicians is another form of coercion. His endorsements are used to control primary candidates, move donors, and deliver institutional appointments. An endorsement withdrawn or withheld has the opposite impact.

Across multiple cycles for many years, Trump has endorsed hundreds of candidates, with an especially strong success rate in party primaries. That influence allows him to trade endorsements for loyalty, policy concessions, or institutional favors later. The endorsements produce political capital that is then spendable—a type of an IOU ledger. As reported on September 13, 2024, on ABC News and *Good Morning America*:

> *Each election cycle since he became president, Trump has endorsed more Senate, House and governor candidates than the one before. . . . And this cycle in particular, Trump's endorsements have taken on a deeper meaning. . . . This year, more than ever before, traditional arms of the Republican Party have practically ceded control of candidate promotion to Trump. . . . It's just the latest example of the Republican Party's transformation into the Party of Trump.*

In economic hit man language: Convert popularity into a credit line of human loyalty. Instead of a loan, you issue an endorsement; instead of interest payments, you expect votes, support or silence, and compliance.

PERSONAL DEBT AS NATIONAL AND INTERNATIONAL STRATEGY

The danger isn't merely that Trump uses these tactics privately. It's that he carries them into national and global policy. The pillar of debt under his administrations has become the foundation for a state model. Loans have been replaced by tariffs. Personal IOUs have been applied to international alliances. Political favors guide foreign policy. The debt trap has risen to the position of an organizing principle of US governance.

Foreign leaders understand this. Most fear it. Some admire it. Alarmingly, more and more try to replicate it. In the classical economic hit man framework, debt is a Trojan horse that smuggles raiders into the fort. Trump plays the role of the leader who rides in on the fabricated horse and directs the invaders.

A less obvious, but vital, currency in Trump's debt ecosystem is the flow of fees—foreign governments and delegations staying at Trump properties, paying for rooms or events that confer access and visibility. Investigative reporting and watchdog analyses have documented foreign payments to Trump properties that created optics and potential leverage (payments for stays, events, and units in Trump World Tower and Washington, DC, hotels). Such revenue is both literal income and symbolic influence: money in the coffers, and lines of access to a president. In the words of a 2024 Citizens for Ethics report:

> *Throughout Donald Trump's time in the White House, he likely benefited from $13.6 million in payments from foreign governments, according to a new analysis by CREW. These payments represent an unprecedented violation of the Constitution's Foreign Emoluments Clause and serve as a reminder of the further violations Trump is poised to bring into office should he return to the White House . . . foreign governments used Trump's businesses to curry favor with him and his administration, while enriching Trump personally.*[29]

Trump is politically indebted to a handful of American billionaires. In 2024, roughly 1 in every 13 dollars spent on national elections was donated by a handful of the country's richest people, totaling over $1 trillion. More than 80 percent of the federal campaign spending by the one hundred wealthiest Americans in 2024 went to Republicans. However, the other side of this equation is that, like the big banks, the billionaires are indebted to Trump. He becomes "too big to fail." They must keep him and his cronies in power.[30]

Money buys access; access buys favors; favors buy policy outcomes. That triangular flow is a personal debt cycle—an economy of gratitude, obligation, expectation, and mutual dependency.

TRUMP'S DEBT DOCTRINE

Debt was my trade. I learned to shape dependence with numbers on a page.

Donald Trump learned to shape dependence with lots of numbers and promises that manipulated the media and people in the United States and around the world—and then he turned those dependencies into power.

Trump's debt doctrine is clear, ruthless, and efficient. It is the modern evolution of the EHM strategy. The language has changed. The tone has changed. The arena has changed. But the architecture—the exploitation of vulnerability to create dependency—remains timeless.

Debt isn't just a financial condition.

Debt is a perception, a state of mind. That was clear to me decades ago while persuading presidents from Ecuador to Indonesia and Argentina to Egypt to accept loans they couldn't repay. We weren't merely indebting their treasuries; by altering their perceptions, we were molding a new reality. We were indebting their spirits.

Trump has taken that same principle and applied it to banks, businesses, political allies, voters, foreign leaders, and entire branches of the US government. The tactics aren't accidental or reactive. They are structural and strategic. They are economic hit man logic scaled to the personality of one man. They are built on the oldest truth of empire-building: A person in debt is a person controlled. A system in debt is a system owned. A nation in debt is a nation dominated.

I once helped write the manual for binding nations to foreign creditors. Trump has written his manual in a different style; he captures the finances, psyches, and money of banks, courts, political parties, and powerful people, as well as the emotions and votes of enough citizens to have won the last election. He blends conventional finance with personal patronage, foreign and domestic cronyism, and legal clemency to create a web of obligations that works like a modern, informal IMF—one that dispenses favors rather than loans, pardons rather than restructurings, endorsements rather than grants.

That web relies on reputation, media spectacle, a captive base, and institutions that tolerate or are weakened enough to accept transactional governance. It is a system of psychological debt, even when it is not always in the form of loans on balance sheets. The liabilities are real: moral, political, legal, and sometimes monetary. And it threatens the very foundations of a system that claims to promote democracy.

6

Pillar #3: Anxiety over Insufficiency

> ***In countries on every continent, I saw how people working for US corporations—though not officially part of the EHM network—participated in something far more pernicious than anything envisioned in conspiracy theories. They would do whatever they thought or were told it would take to perpetuate the system we EHMs advocated. . . .***
>
> ***[T]hese pacts addressed the pillar of anxiety over insufficiency.***
>
> —*CONFESSIONS OF AN ECONOMIC HIT MAN,*
> THIRD EDITION (PAGE 141)

ANXIETY MAY BE CAUSED by insufficiency of food, shelter, and money. But that's not all. It can take many forms.

The New Hampshire boarding school where my dad taught was attended by young men from Africa, Asia, Europe, Latin America, and the Middle East. Beginning when I was four years old, I ate in the school dining room and over the years learned about their backgrounds. All of them were members of the most "successful" families in their countries. Success for them was measured by yardsticks of status that superseded financial wealth: heritage, race, education, and cultural standing. They were the elites. It didn't much matter where their country stood in the GDP rankings.

I became aware of a major change while I was in high school. Economic theories around supply and demand and statistical measurements like GDP, GDP per capita, salaries, and net income were replacing the traditional elitist ideas. Sufficiency was now measured in terms of money. Heritage wasn't as important as access to electricity, highways, ports, airports, mechanized agriculture, and global markets. In other words, the very definition of success was becoming dependent on finances and infrastructure—materialism. If you lived outside the materialistic loop, you lived in a state of anxiety.

The transition was given a boost when President Kennedy created the Alliance for Progress and the Peace Corps. Although they were presented as moral counterweights to Communism, they also functioned as psychological tools that later would serve me in my role as an economic hit man.

DEFINING INSUFFICIENCY

The Alliance for Progress framed poverty as a technical failure. In other words, it was caused by insufficient development, insufficient capital, and insufficient expertise. This narrative implied: "You are poor not because you've been exploited, but because you've failed to develop." People who believe they are "behind" are primed to accept help from those who are "ahead." They turn to foreign experts, foreign corporations, and foreign loans. They acquiesce to mandates from the World Bank, IMF, and other international agencies.

The Peace Corps volunteers I served with in Ecuador (1968–1971) were sincere, idealistic, and compassionate. We all wanted to help. However, we arrived with modern tools, university degrees, good clothes, books, portable radios and tape recorders, and a youthful confidence that was rooted in our own abundance. We inadvertently presented a vision of what "modern" should look like. Although we learned to converse in Spanish, we spoke English among ourselves and offered to teach it to our communities. Local people were hard pressed not to internalize: "Our way is inadequate. We must catch up." They were tempted to ask, "How can *I* become like *them*? How can *I* modernize? How can *I* escape insufficiency?"

The Peace Corps assigned me to an Indigenous community in the Amazon rainforest. Because I was right out of business school, I was sent to a training camp in Southern California, where I learned about credit and savings (C&S) co-ops and to speak rudimentary Spanish. My instructors assured me that helping communities deep in the jungle form C&S co-ops would encourage people to become capitalists and reject Communism.

The literature emphasized that I would be working with some of the most impoverished people on earth. They had no income whatsoever. They were below the World Bank's absolute poverty line.

Once in Ecuador, it took me two days of bone-rattling travel over the top of the Andes Mountains—on a rickety old wooden bus that reeked of mold and sweaty bodies—down the eastern slope and into the steaming rainforest. Then another grueling day of trekking on trails hacked from the jungle that were sometimes knee-deep in viscous mud that sucked at my boots.

Occasionally, I met members of the Shuar tribe (now recognized as a nation within a nation) on the trail. When I tried to practice my lousy Spanish with them, I discovered, to my chagrin, that mine was better than theirs. They spoke Shuar.

My first lesson in US government work: They teach you a language and then send you to a place where nobody speaks it.

Finally, exhausted, disoriented, and depressed, I arrived at the community where I was supposed to spend the next two years. A huge wooden sign on a dilapidated building announced in large red letters: "Built with Alliance for Progress funds."

I was greeted by a grinning man who stepped gingerly through the mud, held out his hand, and announced, "I am Teofilo Mata. You must be our new Peace Corps volunteer." He was the schoolteacher and spoke Spanish.

"Yes," I said, shaking his hand, "I am here to help you with your credit and savings co-op."

His expression was one of open bafflement. "Credit and savings co-op?" He dropped my hand. "What do you mean? Nobody here has any money." He gestured toward the huts scattered around us. "What credit? What savings? You know how it is here: my papayas for your bananas, your milk for my eggs. Credit and savings co-op! No, no. There must be some mistake. We need an agricultural co-op."

My second lesson in US government work: They train you in a skill and send you to a place where nobody can use it.

Resisting a strong desire to dash out of the jungle, take the earliest flight home, and enlist for Vietnam, I stuck it out. After a while, the jungle and the people who welcomed me into their lives grew on me. To my surprise, I discovered that the Shuar were not impoverished. The reports and statistics had been extremely deceptive. These people thrived in close-knit family communities. The forest provided food, shelter, medicine—everything they wanted. Both children and adults played and laughed a great deal. They were a happy and, by all but modern economic measures, a prosperous people.

My third lesson in US government work: Foreigners are categorized by US "experts" who know little about them—other than a few deceptive statistics that trigger biased perceptions.

Much later, I would learn a fourth lesson. A sad and tragic one. Defining that community, as well as the entire country of Ecuador, as impoverished in the 1960s opened the door to exploitation by the military dictatorship that became my client in the 1970s.

In my defense, I have to say that during most of my economic hit man years on the job, I believed I was doing the right thing. I convinced myself that my Peace Corps experience in the rainforest had been an anomaly. I continued to buy into the myth that huge loans used to build massive infrastructure projects raises prosperity for everybody.

However, eventually, as explained in other parts of this book, my actions would come back to haunt me. The guilt over what my country and I had done—and what my government continues to do—would be a major factor in my decision to quit my lucrative job and devote the rest of my life to turning things around.

Today, I know that the loans and infrastructure projects have given Ecuador a higher GDP, more electricity, telephones, computers, stores crammed with consumer goods—and a handful of billionaires and multimillionaires (including the current president). However, the same EHM strategy has plunged over five million people (29 percent of the population) into dire poverty.

Texaco and other international oil companies began drilling in Ecuador's fragile rainforests in 1969. That was the beginning of an era that would empower a new plutocracy in Ecuador and much of Latin America. The oil created collateral for the loans I would help negotiate during the 1970s.

To this day (in 2026), I return to Ecuador every year and am appalled by the horrible impacts of modern development. The area deep in the jungle where I lived as a Peace Corps volunteer is now an ecological disaster, torn apart by a couple of the world's largest copper and gold mines that serve as collateral for Ecuador's massive foreign debts. The trees are gone. The animals have disappeared.

The majority of the Shuar today are truly impoverished. The forests they depended on for food, shelter, and medicines have fallen to the bulldozer. Oil rigs and pit mines scar the landscape. Many Shuar, as well as the Kichwa, Huaorani (also known as Waorani), and other Indigenous neighbors, have been forced to migrate to city slums. Some take the dangerous journey through Central America and into the United States, where they end up in detention camps or prisons, if they survive.

Anxiety over insufficiency is no longer a misleading statistic; it has become a fact of their lives.

WEAPONIZING LANGUAGE

Politicians have learned something critical from the EHM strategy: Anxiety begins with language.

Before debt is imposed, before trade agreements are signed, before resources are extracted, people must first be convinced that they lack sufficiency. They do not have enough material goods. Their land is inadequate. Their homes are too small. Their labor inefficient. Their culture backward. Their future is bleak.

When Trump designates entire nations as "shithole countries" and dismisses people—at home and abroad—as "garbage," he is not merely being crude. At various times he has referred to countries or people as "hellholes," "disgusting," "vermin," and "filthy." In doing so, he is deploying one of the most effective economic hit man tools: the public declaration of insufficiency.

In my days, we cloaked this tactic in technical jargon. We spoke of "underdeveloped economies," "nonviable agricultural systems," "untrainable labor populations," and the "Third World." Trump stripped away the euphemisms and delivered the same message directly, repeatedly, and globally. He characterized the United States as a "dumping ground" for refugees and asylum seekers from other nations.

A country branded as worthless by a US president—whether euphemistically or more bluntly—becomes desperate to prove otherwise. The leaders know that such branding puts them at grave risk. Credit ratings drop. Insurance premiums rise. Diplomatic leverage erodes. Leaders feel exposed—politically. Desperation motivates them to accept unequal trade terms, harsher migration enforcement demands, military cooperation agreements, and resource extraction contracts they would otherwise resist. It is debt-trap logic without the loan. It is a ploy to manipulate anxieties over insufficiency. In the economic hit man world, perception determines worthiness, credit availability, and global status, and perception shapes reality.

Once language reduces people to less than human, policy follows naturally. If countries are garbage, they can be exploited. If communities are hellholes, they can be abandoned. If migrants are invaders, they can be caged. If dissenters are enemies, they can be silenced.

In my work abroad, we never needed to say these things out loud. The numbers said them for us. Trump says them directly—and normalizes them. This normalization is crucial. It lowers moral resistance. It makes cruelty administratively efficient.

GOATS: SYMBOLS OF INSUFFICIENCY

It was easy to emphasize insufficiency to presidents and ministers of finance in countries like Indonesia, Ecuador, Guatemala, and the others that already lacked just about everything the modern world valued. Many of these government officials had graduated from universities in the United States and Europe. They didn't have to be convinced. These were the majority of the countries with resources the United States has targeted during the past five decades. However, there are a few exceptions. Saudi Arabia is an example.

I mentioned earlier that fear was a major factor in convincing the Saudis to accept my deal. Although it may seem contradictory for a country as oil-rich as Saudi Arabia to feel anxiety over insufficiency, encouraging that perception was one of my other tactics. Those two pillars—fear and anxiety over insufficiency—worked hand in hand.

On my first trip to the country in 1974, I watched a herd of goats wandering the streets of Riyadh, the country's capital city, eating garbage that was strewn everywhere. They stank. The garbage stank. The city stank. When I'd previously seen photos of those goats, I'd asked a diplomat what they were doing. I'd been shocked by his response.

"No self-respecting Saudi would ever collect trash," he said. "We leave it to the beasts."

Goats as garbage collectors! In the capital of the world's wealthiest oil kingdom. It seemed preposterous.

But when I actually saw them in person, I realized that the goats were a key to the anxiety over insufficiency strategy. They were a sore point among Saudis jet-setting around the world. Despite all the oil, all the petrodollars, all the influence their country had at OPEC, and despite the undisputed fact that they had brought the United States to its economic knees, they looked to the world like a medieval kingdom that relied on goats as their garbage disposal service.

Every time I met with government officials, I managed to subtly throw in a few words about some aspect of life, in addition to the goats, that highlighted the country's insufficiency—the absence of oil refineries and petroleum-based industries; the unreliable electricity and primitive water, sewage, and educational facilities in much of the country; and ports that were inadequate to handle modern shipping.

The Saudis, unlike officials in poorer countries, tended to be defensive. They fell back on the argument that they had plenty of money and would take care of this problem—which, of course, was exactly what I wanted to hear. My response: Hire us, and we will modernize and defend you.

That anxiety—over reputation, relevance, and loss of face—is the same anxiety economic hit men have cultivated for decades, mostly behind closed doors. Now it is broadcast openly by the US president and politicians from both parties. They call countries out as being insufficient in many ways. Their resources are insufficient. Their economies are insufficient. Their health care is insufficient. Their level of education is insufficient. Their infrastructure is insufficient. The leaders of my client countries were warned that if US-backed development didn't happen fast enough, they would lose their jobs, chaos would follow, and Communists would take over. Today, that same tactic thrives. This sense of urgency is classic economic hit man psychology.

One strategy that in recent years has held special appeal to US administrations is the use of sanctions and tariffs—economic policies that aggravate anxiety over insufficiency. And in many cases the anxiety caused by those policies is totally justified. Although the swords of tariffs and sanctions have been wielded by presidents since George Washington, Trump has thrust them deeper than anyone else—deep enough to slice up the economies of countries on every continent.

Sanctions were a component of foreign policy during Trump's first administration; however, they were often distinct from the use of tariffs targeting certain sectors, including steel (25 percent) and aluminum (10 percent), and specific countries, primarily China (25 percent). In the first year of his second administration, the distinction between tariffs and sanctions blurred, with tariffs explicitly used as a tool to address nontrade, foreign policy issues. The introduction of a universal baseline tariff imposed much higher rates on specific countries—60 percent or more on China, up to 100 percent on Mexico—and rates for other countries that threatened to reach more than 50 percent. Sanctions as a tool to manipulate foreign relations also expanded, particularly around drugs (especially fentanyl) and immigration.[31]

Although these often were only negotiating tactics, by the end of 2025, the threats themselves had dug deep into the global psyche.

THE MESSAGE OF INSUFFICIENCY

In other countries, anxiety over insufficiency dismantles economies and fuels migration. In the United States, it drives people toward authoritarian solutions, away from solidarity, and into subservience to the very forces that make the rich richer, the powerful more powerful, and everybody else more dependent on the greed of those in charge. Furthermore, Trump's threats to impose tariffs and sanctions—and the unpredictability of his follow-through—causes anxiety among US businesses and consumers.

This is not accidental. It is systemic. And it is why language—dismissive, degrading, dehumanizing language—is never just rhetoric. It is economic hit man logic translated into emotional shorthand.

I sat in the office of a top adviser to King Faisal on that first trip to Riyadh.

"You know," he said giving me a condescending smile, "you Americans—all you Westerners—think we're backward. You laugh about our goats. But frankly we have everything we need." He took a sip of tea. "I just flew in my own jet from a vacation on the French Riviera." He set his cup on the ornate table in front of him and glared at me. "Can you do that?"

I returned his smile as politely as I could. "Of course not. You've got more money invested in that jet than I'll ever have."

"You see?"

"But don't you worry about your children and grandchildren?"

"What do you mean?"

"The oil will run out. Then what?"

"They'll have Harvard and Oxford educations."

"And what will they do with those educations?" I went on to say that Saudi Arabia lacked everything a successful country needed: industry, a national and reliable electrical grid, highways, financial and educational institutions, and assets required to convince countries like the United States to defend it against its enemies. I pointed out that those educations would have value only if Saudi's future generations worked for foreign companies—unless they hired us to help them build a viable economy.

The same pillar, planted at different angles, worked in poor and rich countries alike. And also in the United States.

Candidates for US political offices, especially the presidency, repeatedly frame the economy as a zero-sum battlefield. If someone else wins, you lose. If factories close, it's because somebody stole their products or ruined their supply chains. If wages stagnate, it's because others will work for less. There aren't enough jobs. There isn't enough money. There isn't enough safety. There isn't enough energy. There isn't enough respect. There isn't enough of America to go around. And the coup de grâce: Someone else is taking your share.

In classic economic hit man fashion, Trump learned early in life not to question the system itself. As a candidate and as president, he does not criticize corporate consolidation, financialization, or automation. Rather, despite portraying himself as standing for the average American, he protects the big corporations and the oligarchy through deregulation, gerrymandering, and tax reductions for corporations and their owners.

In his first year in the White House, Trump enacted the Tax Cuts and Jobs Act (TCJA) of 2017, which was projected to result in a net tax cut of approximately $1.5 trillion over a ten-year period (2018–2027). In the first year of his second term, he signed the One Big Beautiful Bill Act (OBBBA), a tax law that delivers an estimated $4.5 trillion in tax cuts over ten years and makes many of the tax provisions from the TCJA permanent.

Corporations are the big winners.

The Corporate Tax Rate plummeted from 35 percent to a flat 21 percent. In addition, a new pass-through deduction of 20 percent was granted to qualified owners of pass-through businesses—the vast majority of US businesses. (The profits from such entities "pass through" to their owners' individual income taxes instead of being taxed at the corporate rate.)[32] The net revenue loss from these cuts was projected to be around $1.5 trillion over the decade; the gross tax cuts were estimated at over $5.5 trillion. Medicaid was cut by nearly $1 trillion and billions were trimmed from the Supplemental Nutrition Assistance Program (SNAP).[33]

Cutting back programs like Medicare and SNAP has spinoff effects. Farmers and others who supply food, medicines, and health care services are just a few examples of those who are hurt by budget-depleting social service cuts. These policies result in greater national debt and create more anxiety over scarcity.

Tragically, lower-income people, recipients of assistance programs, and the elderly are the big losers, as are future generations who will suffer from a growing national debt. The rich benefit; the struggling majority suffer.

Many who are hurt by changes in the tax laws and assistance programs have no idea of the damage done to them and to their children, because the administration redirects anxiety outward. The problems, the president says, are caused by former President Biden, Democrats, and anyone else who opposes him. He is the knight in shining armor riding in to save them. For Americans already struggling with debt, job insecurity, health care costs, and declining life expectancy, the spectacle of a domineering personality who will defend them against the treacherous opposition is reassuring.

This is how anxiety over insufficiency metastasizes. People stop asking why the system is failing them and start worrying about being pushed out of it. They cling to identity, borders, and authoritarian promises—not because accepting them actually solves the problems, but because the promises offer psychological shelter from anxiety and humiliation.

The threat is "them"—the others. Migrants, especially, are identified as the bad guys. The Trump administration frames immigration not as a humanitarian issue, but as a flood of criminals who must be stopped to safeguard economic and cultural survival: "They take your jobs." "They drain your benefits." "They attack your values." "They peddle drugs to your kids." "They rape your women." "They cause inflation."

The migrants driven north by economic devastation in Latin America become the villains blamed for insufficiency in the United States. Scarcity is no longer structural. It's personal. And it is someone else's fault.

Whether outside or inside the United States, once anxiety is established, dominion becomes easier. Nations accept unfair trade deals. Workers accept lower or stagnant wages. Communities accept pollution. Citizens accept surveillance, militarization, and repression. People no longer fight for justice. They fight not to be discarded.

This is the final evolution of the EHM strategy. It no longer relies solely on debt instruments or fear. Anxiety of not having enough takes over. The tactics draw on psychological capture—on convincing people that their survival depends on obedience. Once again, Trump did not invent this tactic, but his penchant for acting impulsively turned it into public theater. By transforming contempt into spectacle, he made anxiety contagious. And once anxiety spreads, power concentrates almost effortlessly.

THE ENERGY SCAM

On my first economic hit man assignment, during that gourmet dinner with the rest of my team in the elegant restaurant atop the Hotel InterContinental Indonesia, the role of energy as a tool came through loud and clear.

After describing the importance of oil and of defeating Communism, our project manager, Charlie Illingworth, made a statement that seemed so simple and yet defines an empirical aspect of modern economics. "Electricity is the key," he said. "You can't grow an economy without growing electrical production."

For the next ten years, most of my EHM strategies revolved around convincing targeted nations that they needed to accept massive loans so we could build them modern electric power grids. Instilling anxiety over energy insufficiency was a top tactic.

By the time Trump became president, solar and wind had emerged as more economical than fossil fuels. However, Trump was not buying. He was deeply indebted to an oil industry that had fueled his political ascendancy.

According to a report in *The Guardian*:

> *Big oil spent a stunning $445m throughout the last election cycle to influence Donald Trump and Congress, a new analysis has found.*
>
> *That figure includes funding from January 2023 and November 2024 for political donations, lobbying and advertising to support elected officials and specific policies. Because it does not include money funneled through dark-money groups—which do not have to reveal their donors—it is almost certainly a vast understatement, says the report from green advocacy group Climate Power, which is based on campaign finance disclosures and advertising industry data.*[34]

Trump reciprocated by drawing on the nation's anxieties over scarcity of energy. For many years, Big Oil had spent billions of dollars convincing Americans that oil was a vital and a scarce resource, as well as a symbol of prosperity and economic development. "Peak oil" became a watchword to spread the fear that oil resources had reached their peak and would decline rapidly. We were assured that we would run out of it unless our tax dollars subsidized projects that devastated fragile environments and developed a new industry—fracking.

Trump has persuaded the country to expand drilling, oil pipelines, fracking, and even coal production. He labeled protesters as anti-America and threatened retaliation. Making America great again meant, he maintained, making America the world's number one producer of oil and gas. We had to guard against oil giants like Russia, Iran, and Venezuela. "Drill, baby, drill!" To hell with the economics.

His administration has promoted fossil fuels by rolling back environmental regulations, opening more federal lands to drilling and mining, speeding up pipeline approvals, supporting coal production through subsidies and policy changes, and withdrawing the United States from international climate commitments like the Paris Agreement. Key actions included signing executive orders to remove regulatory barriers, facilitate leasing, and encourage fossil fuel exports.

The Trump White House framed solar and wind not as abundant and affordable but as unreliable risks; it cast fossil fuels as the only dependable lifeline. The implication is clear: Without oil and gas, you will freeze; without coal, your lights will go out; without drilling, civilization collapses. This is classic anxiety over insufficiency conditioning. The fear isn't just about energy—it's about turning control over to a new generation of technologies and "woke" people who can't be trusted. It's about supporting the oligarchy and the one man sitting at the top—the supreme economic hit man.

A study by the Roosevelt Institute concluded:

> *It's no secret that Trump entered office signaling he was a friend to fossil fuel companies. On the campaign trail he'd made them an offer: provide $1 billion to his campaign, and in return, get a wishlist of favorable regulatory fixes. In his first week, he signed EO 14154, "Unleashing American Energy" to remove regulatory barriers to fossil fuel expansion and revoke orders focused on clean energy and environmental justice implemented under the Biden administration. Through this executive order and others, Trump has taken steps to open the Alaskan wilderness to oil drilling, create a new National Energy Dominance Council to expedite approval for fossil fuel projects with limited oversight, roll back regulations on tailpipe emissions, renew the authorization of natural gas export permits, freeze funding allocated by the IRA [Inflation Reduction Act], and direct the attorney general to stop the enforcement of state climate laws deemed potentially unconstitutional or preempted by federal law.*[35]

US crude oil production rose from approximately 8.9 million barrels per day (bpd) in January 2017 to about 11.1 million bpd, a net increase of 2.2 million bpd. At its peak just before the COVID-19 pandemic, US production reached 13.0 million bpd in a single month. Overall, the largest increase in oil production during any presidential term took place under Trump (2.47 bpd).[36]

The focus on fossil fuels lined the pockets of those who owned a doomed industry, and it filled Trump's campaign war chest. It cost American taxpayers a great deal of money, and American workers lost opportunities in the solar and wind industry. Fossil fuels are built on the bones of dinosaurs and today that industry is itself a dinosaur, gasping for breath in the last moments of its death rattle. The unspoken reality is that recent US energy policies have ceded an important economic sector to China.

When Trump first entered the Oval Office, in 2017, the United States led the world in wind power generation. It did not take long for China to turn that around and surpass the United States. China dominated both wind and solar power by 2025. China added more solar in the first half of 2025 than the rest of the world combined, making it the global leader by a huge margin in both total capacity and new installations.[37] Although the United States ranked as number three (behind China and India) for annual installations, most of the added capacity was due to states like Texas, California, Indiana, and Arizona. These states have long histories of oil production dependency; yet, unlike the White House, they recognized that future prosperity depends on switching from fossil fuels to sustainable alternatives.

FROM NATIONS TO MINDS

Trump's most effective insufficiency narrative is not merely economic—it is existential. It is the claim that before him, America was weak, a humiliated loser. This is insufficiency at the level of identity. Just as Saudi Arabia and other nations I exploited were told they were incapable of managing their own resources, Americans are told we are incapable of thriving without an autocrat.

Trump doesn't merely exploit anxiety over insufficiency—he circulates it like money. Much of the media scrambles to repeat

Trump's every insult, lie, or factually challenged claim. Trump's crisis language prevents reflection. Constant emergencies eliminate long-term thinking. When people are anxious, they don't ask structural questions. They don't organize. They don't challenge systems. They follow the leader.

This is the emotional equivalent of debt bondage. Fear replaces interest payments. Loyalty replaces repayment. Obedience replaces rationality. The leader is the creditor. The public is the debtor. Independence is the collateral.

In my economic hit man years, we convinced presidents and dictators that accepting bad deals was the only way to avoid disaster. The system that has evolved in the United States uses the same model on individuals and populations. It has been in play in one form or another for many years, but Trump has incorporated it into his policies and language—as in his "I'm a dictator. But sometimes you need a dictator."[38] His actions and his words tell us that without an authoritarian government, we will lack what we need, and we will be unsafe. This is anxiety over insufficiency personalized.

It is a powerful tactic because it turns perceptions of insufficiency into reality. People can point to real struggles: rising costs, shrinking security, climate disruption, crime, drugs, and technological change. Like NAFTA and CAFTA, the trade agreements that devastated Latin American economies, the current US strategy does not solve scarcity—it manages it. It concentrates benefits upward, enriching the rich, while increasing suffering and fear for everybody else. Economic hit men don't want to eliminate insufficiency. They want to institutionalize it.

The greatest evolution of the EHM strategy is not financial—it is psychological. The strategy I employed in Saudi Arabi proved that. The Saudis didn't need money. They needed to be convinced that they were headed to a future of an insufficiency that went beyond finances. They needed us to persuade people like King Faisal's adviser that only we could offer to relieve them of that anxiety.

The evolution of this EHM strategy has shown that treaties and development loans are not required to create dependence. Just convince people that there is not enough, and that the dictator is the only one who can decide who receives whatever remains. This is the final frontier of empire: controlling perceptions of scarcity instead of resources.

When anxiety over insufficiency governs, freedom contracts. When apprehension replaces trust, the march toward democracy ends. The cost is borne by the many who are taught that there is never enough.

The oligarchy laughs all the way to the bank.

7

Pillar #4: Divide and Conquer

There's no difference between the Republicans and Democrats.

—A COMMON COMPLAINT UNTIL 1995

[Newt] Gingrich became Speaker of the House in January 1995 following an explosion of billionaire money and right-wing media characterizing President Clinton's first two years as corrupt and socialist. He explicitly rejected the traditional view that politicians should work across the aisle for the common good. Instead, he preached that politics should be played like warfare, with enemies and few rules of engagement.

—THOM HARTMANN IN *THE LAST AMERICAN PRESIDENT*[39]

DIVIDE AND CONQUER did not start with Newt Gingrich, but he brought it into "normal" American politics. It has been a roadblock in the path to democracy ever since—one that has piled up, layer upon layer, over time. Under the Trump administration, it has blocked the congressional and judicial branches of government from effectively doing their jobs and vastly increased the power of the executive.

Divide and conquer has been a successful strategy throughout history because it impedes collective strength and turns factions against each other. A large, unified group is hard to defeat. Smaller, competing segments can be bribed, manipulated, and suppressed one at a time. I was very aware that conquering through divisiveness was especially successful when religious, class, ethnic, or regional tensions already existed. We could exploit them to our advantage.

While fear, debt, and anxiety of insufficiency are often based on real physical threats, desires, and needs, divide and conquer draws on psychological elements. It promotes perceptions about the "other"—stories that may be grounded in reality or totally fabricated. Perception—psychological operations (PSYOPs)—plays a major role. Often this pillar binds all four together into a cohesive and highly effective EHM strategy.

In modern US politics, this often translates into tactics such as gerrymandering, propaganda, and the manipulation of racial, religious, and ideological prejudices. Red states versus blue states, rural versus urban, Republican versus Democrat. Trump has augmented these divisive tactics through his extensive use of social media.

Abroad, Trump treats alliances as arenas for fragmentation rather than commitments to collective action. He publicly disparaged the European Union and NATO. He threatened to scale back US defense commitments, forcing individual allies into bilateral bargaining over security instead of encouraging collective defenses. He withdrew the United States from major international agreements, including the Paris climate agreement, the Iran nuclear deal, UNESCO, the Intermediate-range Nuclear Forces Treaty, and the UN Human Rights Council. These decisions came back to haunt him in 2026, when he proclaimed that Iran was developing nuclear weapons and the countries he had alienated refused to join his war.

The divide-and-conquer strategy in the United States has produced a huge gap between the rich and everyone else.

By 2023, the top 1 percent of US households owned 30 percent of US wealth, or 30 cents of every dollar.[40] In September 2025, *Forbes* reported:

> *Another year, another set of broken records for the 400 richest Americans.[41] They're worth a record $6.6 trillion in all, after getting $1.2 trillion richer over the past 12 months. It now takes a record $3.8 billion to make the ranking, $500 million more than the minimum in 2024.*

All this while working families debated whether they could afford groceries and gas in the same week.

During much of my lifetime, wealthy dynasties like the Rockefellers (oil), Mellons (oil and aluminum), Hunts (oil), and Fords (cars) downplayed their riches. They might run for political office or praise themselves as philanthropists, but they did not parade their lifestyles. They did not want to be seen as different, divisive.

This had changed by 2025, when Musk, Bezos, Zuckerberg, and a handful of other billionaires joined Trump on the stage during his second inauguration. The tech giants flaunt their wealth and excessive obsession with materialism: their super yachts, super planes, and super mansions. They have divided themselves from the rest of the world, which they see as a resource to be exploited.

This "great divide" was not entirely lost on the American public. As reported in *The New York Times*:

> *According to the most recent edition of an annual Harris Poll, for the first time, a majority of Americans believe billionaires are a threat to democracy. A remarkable 71 percent believe there should be a wealth tax. A majority believe there should be a cap on how much wealth a person can accumulate.[42]*

TRUMP'S PLAYBOOK AND ITS ECONOMIC HIT MAN PARALLELS

Trump has implemented a record-breaking torrent of EHM strategies designed to divide and conquer populations everywhere. Table 1 is not comprehensive—the full catalog would fill volumes—but it illustrates the pattern with devastating clarity.

TABLE 1: Mapping Trump's Tactics to EHM Strategies

TRUMP'S TACTIC	EHM PARALLEL	PURPOSE
Framing immigrants as criminals, invaders, and drains on scarce resources.	In Latin America, we routinely blamed poverty and instability on local populations—corruption, laziness, overpopulation, or backwardness—rather than on debt structures imposed by foreign lenders.	Redirect anger downward and sideways, never toward the architects of colonialism and extraction.
Weaponizing race, gender, religion, and culture to fracture coalitions.	In countries like Indonesia, Ecuador, and Guatemala, we exploited ethnic, tribal, and religious divisions to weaken resistance to large infrastructure and resource deals.	Divide the populace so they cannot organize against dictatorial leaders.
Declaring emergencies—crime, drugs, border crossings, moral collapse—to expand executive power.	We exaggerated or engineered events that forced governments into emergency IMF and World Bank loans and divided public opinion.	Generate crisis to suspend skepticism and drive people to follow the leader.
Labeling journalists, scientists, educators, judges, and critics as enemies or traitors.	We portrayed leaders who questioned debt deals or neoliberal reforms—like Jaime Roldós and Omar Torrijos—as unstable, corrupt, and dangerous.	Isolate truth-tellers and opponents before neutralizing them.

TRUMP'S TACTIC	EHM PARALLEL	PURPOSE
Blaming foreign nations, migrants, or trade partners for domestic economic pain.	We framed austerity and unemployment as the unavoidable result of global markets or foreign competition, not rigged financial systems.	Hide structural exploitation behind external villains.
Rolling back climate protections and prioritizing fossil fuel extraction.	Throughout Africa and Latin America, we pressured resource-rich nations to ignore environmental devastation in exchange for loans and short-term growth.	Sacrifice long-term sustainability for immediate profit—benefiting corporations, not citizens.
Granting clemency to the January 6 rioters and deploying or threatening to deploy military and federal forces to US cities.	When economic pressure failed abroad, we relied on jackals—coups, military intimidation, or covert actions—to force change, as in Chile, Guatemala, Iran, and Panama.	Cause friction and disputes among people who might otherwise unite to solve structural problems.
Restructuring courts, agencies, and foreign and civil services to ensure ideological loyalty.	We pushed many nations into constitutional rewrites, trade agreements, privatization mandates, and regulatory dismantling to lock in corporate control that would continue long after leaders left office.	Make extraction and other pro–big business policies permanent, not dependent on elections.
Using dehumanizing language like "vermin," "garbage," and "shithole countries."	We relied on propaganda portraying certain nations, cultures, or individuals as inferior, incapable of governance, dangerous, or undeserving of sovereignty or public office.	Create antagonism toward specific groups, countries, and people and make exploitation morally palatable.
Threatening to take over Greenland and Canada and thereby proclaiming the United States's right to occupy any country the president wants.	We made our job much easier in Saudi Arabia by highlighting US threats to invade the country and Kuwait after the 1973 oil embargo.	Scare countries into submission and/or improve negotiation positions.

DIVIDING THE SHUAR

The Shuar were the first Indigenous people I ever knew. I arrived in their territory in the late 1960s as a Peace Corps volunteer—young, idealistic, and utterly unprepared for what I would witness over the next three years and during the following decades.

As I wrote earlier, the majority of the Shuar today live in poverty, their ancestral forests bulldozed and replaced by oil rigs and pit mines. But deep in the rainforest, in a region classified as the Sacred Headwaters of the Amazon, a united group of communities has been fighting to preserve both their homeland and their way of life.

In the early 1990s, I cofounded with Bill and Lynne Twist the Pachamama Alliance, a nonprofit dedicated to supporting the Shuar, Achuar, and their neighbors while learning from them about "changing the destructive dream of the industrialized world." We helped pressure Ecuador's government to adopt a new constitution guaranteeing Indigenous communities the right to "free, prior, and informed consent." At least in theory, no project could proceed without genuine consultation and agreement from affected communities.

A major copper deposit was discovered in the Sacred Headwaters in 2000, but the Shuar refused consent. They organized direct, on-the-ground resistance to physically prevent mining personnel from accessing sites; formed alliances; and initiated legal challenges.

In 2019 Solaris Resources, a Canadian-Chinese joint venture, acquired the project. And the EHM divide-and-conquer playbook opened once again.

A powerful coalition formed: Canadian and Chinese mining interests, Ecuadorian government officials hungry for revenue, and—tacitly—the US embassy and international mining and oil lobbies. Their goal was simple: Break the Shuar's unity and gut the constitutional protections that stood in their way.

In the summer of 2024, Bill Twist and I traveled to Macas, the provincial capital. We met with Domingo Ankuash, the democratically elected president of the Shuar Governing Council, and his supporters, who remained committed to stopping the mining operations. They handed us a statement from the Alliance of Human Rights Organizations in Ecuador, dated July 23, 2024. It stated (in part and translated):

> *The Alianza de Organizaciones de Derechos in Ecuador denounces that early this morning, at least 100 uniformed National Police officers entered (without a court order) the headquarters of the Federation of Shuar Centres (FICSH) in Sucúa, Morona Santiago. They evicted the President of the Governing Council, led by Domingo Ankuash, and ten others who were with him. . . .*
>
> *The current FICSH leadership has been prevented from entering the building. The person who has been granted access is the former president, David Tankamash.*
>
> *This incident is the latest in a series of events that have significantly impacted the Shuar federation and its practice of self-governance. Tankamash was removed from the presidency of the FICSH for ignoring the decisions made in assembly to protect Shuar territory and life, which is under serious threat by mining extractivism.*[43]

No warrant. A police raid that installed a former official who had been removed for betraying his people. This was divide and conquer in its purest form.

During our meetings, we heard descriptions of tactics that came straight from the pages I could have written myself decades earlier.

A "feasibility study," similar to the ones I had conducted for Ecuador's military dictatorship in the 1970s, had been produced. It enumerated the supposed benefits the mine would bring to national and local economies while conveniently omitting the catastrophic impacts to the environment and Indigenous cultures.

The mining coalition launched a propaganda campaign throughout Ecuador portraying opposition to the mine as unpatriotic, criminal, and treasonous. Economic hit men fanned out across Shuar territory offering chain saws, backhoes, and "salaries" to anyone who would support the mining project. They promised schools and infrastructure. People who falsely claimed to represent their communities signed consent documents granting Solaris permission to proceed. The divisions were often generational; the older, more traditional Shuar opposed the project, while the younger generations were more easily influenced by money and infrastructure projects.

Classic. Textbook. Devastating.

FIRE ON THE MOUNTAIN

Bill and I sat at a restaurant on the outskirts of Macas with Ankuash and his supporters, listening to their accounts of betrayal and resistance. We drank exotic fruit juices while I tried to drive the dark thoughts from my mind—guilt about my own role in developing the strategies now being deployed against these people, dread about what was coming.

Through the window, I could see the magnificent Upano River, its waters originating in glaciers atop the cloud-shrouded Andes—glaciers that are rapidly vanishing due to the global warming that the EHM strategy accelerates.

As we talked, the clouds began to lift. Slowly at first, then more rapidly.

Narcissa, a Shuar leader and friend for more than thirty years, sucked in her breath. "Look!" she gasped, pointing.

The receding mists revealed Sangay—a spectacular cone-shaped volcano usually hidden by the heavy clouds where warm Amazonian air collides with glacial Andean winds. Mushroom-like billows of dark smoke and flashes of fire erupted into the sky.

We sat transfixed. Speechless.

Finally, Ankuash spoke, his voice quiet with reverence: "Even we who live here are seldom treated to this."

He paused, watching the mountain breathe fire.

"The spirit of the mountain is speaking. Pachamama, Mother Earth, is telling us that we must protect her. We must persevere."

In that moment, I renewed my vow to continue focusing my knowledge of the economic hit man system on exposing and dismantling it, even as the system and the people who uphold and benefit from it seem more determined than ever to drive the human race toward self-destruction.

The 2024 elections loomed. Biden had stumbled badly during his recent debate with Trump. Trump was surging toward a second term. What would this mean for the Shuar? For Ecuador? For all of us?

In November of 2025, Solaris announced that it had advanced from exploration to development. A press release projected over three hundred thousand tons of copper equivalent per year, plus molybdenum, gold, and silver and average annual earnings of $1.9 billion in the first five years.

The press release claimed the project was "underpinned by a strong and structured social foundation, built through formal agreements, inclusive dialogue, and shared value creation with Indigenous communities and local stakeholders."[44]

It didn't mention that those agreements were signed by people the Shuar did not recognize as legitimate representatives.

Soon after the press release, the company began carving roads through fragile jungle that opened the entire region to colonists, lumber companies, and cattle ranches. Huge machines savagely gutted one of the most biodiverse ecosystems on Earth—the essential headwaters of the Amazon River Basin watershed.

People, plants, animals, cultures, and the global climate were being ripped apart.

In the end, we will all pay the price.

COMBATING UNITY

Economic hit men learn early that unity is the enemy.

A united population asks questions. It organizes resistance. A divided one accepts deals because it's too busy fighting itself to challenge the outsiders. In my years, I rarely needed to threaten leaders directly. Instead, I exploited fractures—ethnic, regional, ideological, class-based. When people disagreed with each other, they stopped resisting the system that exploited them all.

Divide and conquer wasn't merely a tactic. It was an essential part of the overall strategy—an integrating force supporting the other three pillars.

At its core, the strategy is simple:

1. Identify fault lines within a society—immigrant communities, urban residents, external nations, educational systems, cultural minorities, and other perceived threats to economic security and national identity.

   For example: In Colombia, we pitted subsistence farmers whose lands were flooded by hydroelectric dams against the urban rich who benefited from the electricity. One of the unintended consequences of this was the formation of right-wing paramilitary forces and Marxist guerilla groups like FARC—and ultimately, violent turf wars waged around narco-trafficking, blackmailing, and extortion.

2. Amplify fear and resentment on both sides through narratives of us versus them (law-abiding versus criminal, insider versus outsider, traditional values versus ideological "others") and initiate policy battles that deepen social fractures.

   In Guatemala, it was the Mayan people who believed their rivers, hot springs, and forests were sacred versus Big Agriculture, including the United Brands Company (originally the United Fruit Company and currently Chiquita

Brands International), and its determination to turn those lands into banana plantations.

3. Personalize blame—don't identify systemic causes; instead redirect public attention away from structural inequality, corporate monopolization, and wealth concentration.

   Across Latin America, we accused individuals like Allende of Chile, Roldós of Ecuador, and Torrijos of Panama of being Soviet puppets intent on destroying capitalism. We attacked them personally, thus deflecting blame away from the structural problems that caused severe inequality, poverty, and injustice.

4. Position yourself as the only hope—emphasize your successes, never admit to failure, don't be encumbered by the truth, and paint the opposition as incompetent, stupid, and even treasonous.

   In the three countries just mentioned, we launched propaganda campaigns portraying those individuals as treasonous and promised that, by getting rid of them, we would lead their countries into prosperity through neoliberal economics and our "development" programs.

5. Extract power by centralizing and personalizing institutions and destroying resistance—reorganize government agencies, the judiciary, the educational system, and the military; demonstrate your power by bullying anyone who resists, including weaker countries and the media.

   This happened in nearly every country where I worked. It was most obvious in Iran, where we helped keep the shah in power for many years through the CIA-trained and extremely brutal secret police/intelligence agency SAVAK. Every institution in the country, from judicial to military, understood that it had to bow to the demands of the shah and SAVAK.

The goal is never to resolve conflict; the goal is to manage it. Divide and conquer works by ensuring that the public contends with internal and external enemies, rather than confronting the architecture of control that shapes economic and political outcomes. Those in power are not portrayed as an oligarchy; they are the cavalry riding in to save the day.

THE PSYCHOLOGY OF FRACTURE

Divide and conquer works because it exploits something fundamental about human psychology: We are tribal by nature. We instinctively identify with groups and view outsiders with suspicion. Under stress, this tendency intensifies. Fear makes us contract. We cling to those who look, sound, and think like us—while pushing the "other" away.

When populations are divided, they surrender oversight. They tolerate corruption. They accept inequality as inevitable. They stop asking who benefits from their suffering and start blaming each other instead.

These mechanisms generate a political environment in which collective grievance overwhelms structural critique. Populations become easier to influence, easier to command, and easier to distract from the true architects of their misery.

The people live in a trance of denial. Wealth flows upward. The system doesn't just survive—it thrives.

Every president in my lifetime has used some version of this pillar. For Kennedy, it was Communism versus democracy. For Johnson, the anti–Vietnam War "peaceniks" versus the pro-war "patriots." For Bush 2, the post-9/11 "you're with us or against us" mantra. For Biden, MAGA versus "mainstream" Americans.

Trump refined this strategy for a domestic audience and deployed it with unprecedented ferocity.

What makes his version distinct is its brazen visibility. Trump didn't just use it; he flaunted it. Economic hit men once worked in the shadows—pitting ministries against each other, rewarding elites while marginalizing the masses. Trump spotlighted it, exposing the strategy to the public arena. During the first year of his second term, the divide-and-conquer strategy became the organizing principle of American government. Trump has deployed a relentless barrage of policies and executive actions designed to intensify social fractures and redirect attention away from questions of power, inequality, and accountability.

OPERATION CONDOR

My economic hit man work in Latin America took me across the continent—to Argentina, Brazil, Chile, Colombia, Costa Rica, Ecuador, Guatemala, Panama, and Venezuela. I maintained an office in Colombia that served as the headquarters for my operations on that continent throughout much of the 1970s.

By the time I joined the economic hit man ranks in 1971, it had become evident that the United States had lost Vietnam. Ecuadorians and other Latin Americans celebrated this as an ignominious US defeat. The empire could be beaten. In response, the Johnson and Nixon administrations claimed that the Soviets were using Cuba to launch terrorists throughout the hemisphere. They enlisted the help of Chile and Argentina—countries with deep fascist traditions.

In 1975, Chile hosted a meeting of six dictatorships: Argentina, Bolivia, Brazil, Chile, Paraguay, and Uruguay. They formed what became known as Operation Condor. Ecuador and Peru would later join.

Divide and conquer was the cornerstone strategy. The dictators launched brutal campaigns against anyone advocating for better working conditions, health care, fair wages, or human rights. They turned citizens against the very institutions designed to protect them. They criminalized opposition leaders as Soviet spies.

When Chuck Noble and I visited Argentina in the late 1970s, we were there because MAIN was engineering the huge Salto Grande hydroelectric project. However, as a retired major general who hated Communists and had overseen US engineering projects in Vietnam, Chuck became an informal adviser to the Argentine generals. At first, I couldn't understand why he liked me and treated me like a son; I saw myself as a draft-resisting ex–Peace Corps volunteer.

Then one morning over breakfast in a Buenos Aires hotel, he looked me squarely in the eye and said, "You know, I admire you for joining the Peace Corps and spending three years in the jungles and mountains of Ecuador. That took incredible courage. You didn't have an army at your back. You were out there alone. And you were spreading capitalism in a part of the world that needs it."

That afternoon we were driven to a military base outside Buenos Aires, where we met with a dozen or so Argentine generals and admirals. Chuck was asked to talk about the lessons he had learned in Vietnam.

"You must do everything you can to prevent your enemies from being organized," he told his audience. "Pit their various factions and leaders against each other. They are not part of a disciplined chain of command like your military. You can be sure there are jealousies and power struggles. Do everything you can to foment disagreement, discontent, and rivalries." He glanced around the room. "Divide and conquer. It's as old as the ages and every bit as effective today as it was during Julius Caesar's time."

Those words would haunt me for decades.

I was shocked years later to learn the full scale of Operation Condor's carnage: sixty to eighty thousand South Americans killed or "disappeared." An estimated four hundred thousand imprisoned or tortured.[45] Learning this contributed to my determination to write the *Confessions* trilogy.

Operation Condor's divide-and-conquer tactics cast a shadow across the entire continent that persists to this day.

GUNBOAT DIPLOMACY RETURNS

Between August and October 2025, Trump dispatched a massive flotilla of warships, including the world's largest aircraft carrier, to the Caribbean. He claimed it was to combat "narco-terrorism." However, many believed that the real goal was to take President Maduro and capture the country's oil fields. The unprecedented display of military power generated a great deal of discord at home and around the world—especially in Latin America. Was this really about drugs? Or was it just the first step toward invading Panama and taking the Panama Canal and then moving on to Colombia, Ecuador, and other South and Central American countries to commandeer their oil, gold, copper, and rare minerals?

I was shocked by this spectacle. In all my years as an economic hit man, I had never witnessed anything even remotely approaching it in magnitude. Previous large-scale Caribbean deployments during the 1962 Cuban Missile Crisis, the 1965 Dominican Republic intervention, and the 1980s military buildup in Honduras had been much smaller and ostensibly justified as protecting the hemisphere against the Soviet Union. The CIA had been involved in coups against a number of governments, but nothing that compared to this immense show of force. And against narco-traffickers, as opposed to the Soviet Union! However, it did bring to mind Chuck Noble's advice that afternoon in Argentina: "Do everything you can to foment disagreement, discontent, and rivalries."

In September 2025, the US military flotilla launched strikes on small boats in the Caribbean and Pacific—asserting that the occupants were smuggling drugs. The campaign killed at least 115 people. It sparked international legal challenges, with families of victims claiming their loved ones were fishermen rather than drug smugglers. Lawyers pointed out that the United States does not have the legal authority to use lethal force against alleged drug traffickers in international waters.

"Gunboat diplomacy!" headlines screamed across Central and South America and throughout the Caribbean. Latin American social media overflowed with "Gringo, Go Home," "No more Yankees," "Down with the Monroe Doctrine" messages.

Brazilian President Lula da Silva's adviser Celso Amorim warned, "We cannot accept an outside intervention because it will trigger immense resentment. It could inflame South America and lead to radicalization of politics on the whole continent."[46]

Speaking at the UN General Assembly, Colombia's president, Gustavo Petro, condemned the attacks and called for an investigation into Trump and other US officials involved in the strikes. "Launching missiles over two people in a small boat is a war crime," Petro told CBS News.[47]

On January 3, 2026, it became apparent that the suspicions about Trump's desire to control Venezuela were correct. US forces captured President Maduro and his wife, Cilia Flores, in a military operation that involved roughly 200 Special Operations forces and 150 aircraft. They brought Maduro to the United States to face federal narco-terrorism and drug trafficking charges. Although many Latin Americans disliked Maduro, they condemned the use of such a massive "invasion"—one that killed at least fifty Venezuelan and Cuban military personnel.

Shortly after Maduro's capture, Trump announced his true intentions. "We will run the country until such time as we can do a safe, proper and judicious transition. We can't take a chance that someone else takes over Venezuela. . . ."[48]

He continued, "This Oil will be sold at its Market Price, and that money will be controlled by me, as President of the United States of America." His words begged the question: What right does a US president have to "run" another country and personally control the money earned from selling its most valuable resource?[49]

On top of all this, Trump refused to throw his support behind the country's opposition leader, Maria Machado (despite accepting the gift of her Nobel Prize), and instead kept Maduro's vice president and other top aides in power. A classic divide-and-conquer maneuver, it threw Venezuelans—and the world—off-balance and rendered the opposition impotent.

I was in Ecuador with a film crew that was making a documentary about economic hit men and my role as one from January 9 to 18, 2026. When some of my Latin American friends referred to Trump's actions as "the Caribbean Blitzkrieg," it took me back to books I'd read about infamous potentates of history—from Genghis Khan and Alexander the Great to Hitler. During interviews with the filmmakers, I suffered pangs of guilt once again as I relived, on camera, my role in helping to develop the modern version of the four pillars that now formed the foundation of Trump's policies.

The massive military buildup deepened old fractures and opened new ones—between governments and populations, between left and right, between those who would accommodate Washington and those who would resist.

Even the leaders of nations who agreed on the outcome—ending Maduro's rule—were divided over the methods. Right-wing governments in Argentina and Ecuador supported the US action. Left-wing governments in Brazil and Colombia vehemently opposed it. Within the United States and countries around the world, the deployment drove wedges between political factions that should have been allies. Many asked: If it could happen there, why not anywhere? If Venezuela today, why not us tomorrow?

In Venezuela itself, opposition sectors that should have united instead split between those who pandered to Trump and those who rejected his actions as a return to imperialism.

Divide and conquer. As old as the ages. As effective as ever.

THE HOME FRONT: PART 1

At home, Trump fell back on an old scapegoat: immigrants. By framing them as job stealers, criminals, and cultural threats, he redirected anger away from offshoring corporations, union busting, deregulation, and financialization of the economy. The ensuing discord successfully transformed what was formerly a policy debate about labor markets and legal status into an emotion-packed panic that was extremely divisive.

The immigration debates draw attention away from structural questions: automation, wage stagnation, corporate consolidation, the metastasizing oligarchy. Conversations about health care, education, vaccinations, the Epstein files, debt, tariffs and other trade agreements, the accumulation of personal wealth by the Trump family, and climate change vanish under the weight of cultural warfare.

Then, another watershed moment.

On January 7, the day before I'd headed to Latin America, an ICE agent, Jonathan Ross, fatally shot Renée Good, a thirty-seven-year-old writer, poet, US citizen, and mother in Minneapolis. According to accounts, Good was in her car when Ross approached, and after she briefly reversed and then began moving forward, Ross fired three shots while standing at the front left of her vehicle as it turned away from him. This incident sparked immediate controversy, with federal officials claiming Good was attempting to run over the agent and Minneapolis mayor Jacob Frey, after viewing the video footage, denouncing ICE's claims as lies and demanding that its agents leave the city.

Reading news bulletins on my cell phone as I sat in airports and on airplanes, it seemed more than coincidence that Trump was taking actions in the United States that, like a surreal movie, reflected those in the Caribbean—as though his success at capturing Maduro had emboldened him to invade Minneapolis and other cities in his own country. Heavily armed and masked ICE agents smashed car windows, yanked people from vehicles, and conducted what many believed to be illegal door-to-door operations. It was an unprecedented domestic militarized operation.

ICE had been brutally active in Chicago and Los Angeles in 2025, peaking with Operation Midway Blitz (for Blitzkrieg?) in Chicago in September. These actions prompted protests and the deployment of the National Guard in Los Angeles. But, as with so many of Trump's actions, things continued to escalate. Now, as I returned to Ecuador, the country where it had all started for me, I felt a deep sense of shame for my own country.

I had first come to Ecuador as a Peace Corps volunteer who openly resisted being drafted to fight in a war I opposed, yet I was accepted to work for a US peace agency. Later I had returned as an economic hit man and then as an advocate for Indigenous and environmental rights against foreign resource extraction companies. During all those years, I had felt that, despite our faults, we in the United States had something to offer the world—something I'd later call the American Ideal, a model for a Global Ideal. Now Trump's economic hit man presidency was totally shattering that ideal.

An Ecuadorian friend handed me a newspaper report that described how ICE agents had fired flash-bang grenades and chemical agents into crowds of peaceful protesters. "Can this be true?" he asked. "In the Land of the Free?" I had to admit that, as unbelievable as it seemed, it was true.

The film crew that traveled to Ecuador included thirteen people. They came from England, France, Spain, and Latin America, in addition to the United States. During conversations, ICE was often referred to as "Trump's private paramilitary," "vigilantes," "Trump's Brownshirts" (a reference to Hitler's paramilitary), "goons," and "gangster mercenaries." Someone suggested that the Ku Klux Klan had taken over the White House. These were sobering discussions. Deeply disturbing.

The economic hit man presidency was painting a picture of the United States that no one had previously believed possible. The idea of making America great again had turned a country I loved into a global pariah.

One of the thirteen people was my eighteen-year-old grandson, Grant. I had dedicated the second book in the *Confessions of an Economic Hit Man* trilogy "to my grandson, Grant Ethan Miller, who inspires me to do whatever it takes to create a world he and his brothers and sisters across the planet will want to inherit." I was grateful that he was seeing Ecuador and meeting Indigenous people who had inspired me. I could only hope that, despite what was happening in his country, this trip would inspire him to work toward reinvigorating the American Ideal and taking it out to the world.

THE HOME FRONT: PART 2

By the time Grant and I returned to the United States, the social and economic disruptions in Minneapolis and elsewhere had mushroomed: Schools had transitioned to remote learning, visits to local food pantries had dropped drastically, and restaurants and stores had shuttered. People across the country were scared.

On January 23, thousands participated in a Minnesota statewide general strike with over six hundred businesses closing in what organizers called an "economic blackout" demanding "no work, no school, no shopping."

Then, on January 24, ICE agents killed thirty-seven-year-old Alex Pretti, an ICU nurse at the Minneapolis VA. Minnesota Governor Tim Walz denounced federal claims that Pretti had pulled a gun on agents as "nonsense" and "lies." Walz's denunciation was substantiated by videos taken at the scene. Federal agents blocked Minnesota Bureau of Criminal Apprehension personnel from entering the scene even though they had a court-signed search warrant.

Columnist Julian E. Zelizer summed up the reaction of many Americans in *Foreign Policy*: "The horror of watching a U.S. citizen die at the hands of federal or state officials transcends ordinary politics. Such a ruthless deployment of power not only evokes deep and widespread human emotion but also collides directly with fundamental U.S. values rooted in the Constitution."[50] It was hard to see the Minneapolis operation as anything but a war against the American people.

I can only guess at what the future may bring, but I am certain that the United States will never be the same and that those videos will not allow the world to forget—at least not during my lifetime and probably not during my grandson Grant's. I am reminded of the Shakespearian quotes I had recited to myself during my economic hit man years: "What's done is done," and "What's done can't be undone."

Together, the "Caribbean Blitzkrieg" and the attack on American cities divided the United States perhaps even more deeply than during the Vietnam War. After all, neither the US invasion of Venezuela nor the ICE attacks on US citizens were a war against Communists or a foreign army.

IRAN

Then came the attack on Iran (officially the Islamic Republic of Iran). In late February 2026, the United States and Israel launched a sweeping joint military campaign that marked one of the most consequential ruptures in American foreign policy in generations.

This was a war against a foreign army. It also evoked memories of anti-Communist rhetoric with references to "the radical Islamic regime" and "religious lunatics." To many Americans, it may have seemed similar to the invasion of Venezuela. However, it reminded me of the 1960s and 1970s, when Washington used ideological propaganda and military arguments to justify the war in Vietnam, Operation Condor, and other acts of aggression.

The strikes highlighted a conflict that Trump himself had helped set in motion. His administration had withdrawn from the Iran nuclear deal in 2018. After hitting Iran's nuclear facilities in

June 2025, he insisted that the nuclear program was "obliterated," yet he waged a far larger war just eight months later over the same alleged nuclear threat. Even some of Trump's supporters, including media influencers like Tucker Carlson and Megyn Kelly, began to question the logic behind some of the administration's actions.

The attack exposed a profound contradiction at the heart of Trump's second term. A president who had won the White House twice by campaigning against "forever wars" and promising to keep America out of new conflicts had now waged what could become the most destabilizing war the Middle East has seen in decades—a war with the potential to involve much of the rest of the world.

Whether the conflict ends quickly or drags on, its consequences for regional stability, global energy markets, American credibility, and the future of nuclear nonproliferation are certain to reverberate long after the last missile falls. And it has divided the United States in ways that likely will have a profound impact on future presidents and their foreign policies.

As I watch this war unfold, I can only imagine how it is going over with China's Xi and Russia's Putin. Despite causing supply chain disruptions and other short-term problems for their economies, when they contemplate the long run and the ways this war has divided the American people and their allies, they must be rubbing their hands together in glee.

WHY DIVIDE AND CONQUER WORKS

Divide and conquer succeeds because it transforms politics from a contest of ideas into a battle of identities. When people are told repeatedly that "others"—not systems—are the cause of their hardships, they focus on rivalry rather than the structural arrangements shaping their lives.

Regardless of future events, Venezuela, Minneapolis, and Iran are symbols that will endure. They have redefined the very character of the US government. They have exposed fundamental weaknesses in the American system. They have proven beyond the shadow of a doubt that the Oval Office can be inhabited by a ruthless economic hit man. They have attempted to render populations incapable of unified resistance. They have distracted us from challenging the real sources of our problems.

Every economic hit man operates from the knowledge that a divided population creates dependency. People locked in conflict seek protection. They rally around autocrats. They accept authoritarian measures in exchange for reassurance. They surrender freedoms they once thought inalienable.

8

Changing Perceptions and Manifesting the Global Ideal

AS I WROTE IN THE INTRODUCTION, this book is not just about Donald Trump.

Yes, his name appears on nearly every page. Yes, I've documented how he deployed the four pillars of the EHM strategy—fear, debt, anxiety over insufficiency, and divide and conquer—with unprecedented visibility and aggression. But Trump is a symptom, not the disease. He is the latest and most extreme manifestation of an economic hit man system that has failed to support the American Ideal for decades. He is the embodiment of the economic hit man presidency.

His presidency will terminate.

The question that matters now is: How do we create a country that honors the American Ideal and turn it into a Global Ideal?

THE GLOBAL IDEAL

When I speak of the Global Ideal, I mean something specific: the set of principles that once was known as the American Ideal because it defined this country's highest aspirations. Liberty with responsibility. Equality. Justice. Democracy. Opportunity. An individualism that supports and strengthens family and community. Ever since the founding of this nation, those principles have appealed to people all over the world. Regardless of how they feel about the US government's policies and relationship to their country, they desire to live with those principles. Those values embody the Global Ideal.

Ironically, these principles have never been fully realized in the United States. The Founders who wrote "all men are created equal" also enslaved human beings. The nation that promised opportunity also built wealth on land stolen from Indigenous nations and exploited labor. The democracy that inspired the world also denied the vote to women and Black citizens, gave corporate CEOs tremendous power over elections, and fomented an oligarchy of billionaires.

But in the United States the Ideal has persisted. It serves as a north star—a guide toward a worthy destination. Past generations measured themselves against that standard and expanded its reach. The abolitionists. The suffragettes. The labor movement. The civil rights marchers. The environmentalists. The protesters against ICE. Generations of men and women who fought in wars and died to defend that Ideal.

Progress was never inevitable. Americans worked for these ideals, bled for them, wrote about them, and sang about them. Teachers taught these ideals in schools. Congress and the courts protected these ideals. Americans have honored these ideals at most sporting events, facing the flag as they listen to "The Star-Spangled Banner." And the Ideal was always under threat from those who benefited from the gap between it and the realization of their exploitative ambitions.

The economic hit man system is the architect of that gap.

BEYOND PARTISANSHIP

Let's be clear: The economic hit man presidency is not a partisan issue.

Democrats and Republicans alike have served it. Clinton championed trade deals that hollowed out American manufacturing. Obama bailed out Wall Street while Main Street drowned. Biden's administration, for all its rhetoric about the middle class, left the fundamental structures of oligarchy intact.

The system doesn't care which party holds power. It cares only that power serves its interests.

Trump's innovation was to stop pretending. Previous administrations maintained the fiction that government served the people while in fact it quietly primarily benefited the oligarchy. Trump dropped the mask. He has installed billionaires in his cabinet, granted them unprecedented advantages, and celebrated greed as virtue. He shouts words that were once only whispered. His idea of making America great again means making the wealthy stronger than ever.

In doing so, he has revealed what had been true all along.

So, back to the question we must ask ourselves. It is not simply whether to support or defeat Trump—or any other politician. The question is: How do we dismantle a system that produces oligarchy instead of democracy, and how do we build something worthy of the Global Ideal in its place?

THE POWER OF PERCEPTION

Throughout this book, I've emphasized a truth that proponents of the economic hit man system understand better than most of us: Perception motivates actions; actions shape reality.

This isn't philosophy or mysticism. It's mechanics.

When we perceive billionaires as heroes and job creators, we grant them tax breaks, deregulation, and political access. When we perceive them as oligarchs extracting wealth from the commons, we demand accountability, fair taxation, and democratic constraint. The billionaires haven't changed. Our perception has.

When we perceive immigrants as threats, we build walls and detention centers. When we perceive them as neighbors and hard workers, we build communities and shared prosperity. The immigrants themselves haven't changed. Our perception has.

With those changes in perception come new actions—and a new reality.

The economic hit man system is, at its core, a perception management operation. Fear, debt, scarcity, division—each pillar works by shaping how we see the world. PSYOPs, as I noted earlier, is the military term. But it's not confined to military operations. It saturates our media, our politics, our culture, and our daily lives.

The current dominant perception can be summarized simply: Promote extreme materialism and demand deferment to power.

Americans have been taught to measure success by how much we can accumulate. Bigger houses, newer cars, more stuff. We've been trained to admire the wealthy simply for being wealthy—to assume that riches signal intelligence or divine favor. We've been educated to see those in power as naturally deserving of power, and to see ourselves as subordinate.

This perception serves the EHM strategy perfectly. It turns us into compliant consumers and docile citizens. It encourages us to compete against each other for crumbs while the feast happens next door. It drives us to worship the very people who exploit us. Republicans and Democrats may be locked in divisive battles of disagreement, but during my lifetime both have empowered the oligarchy, at the expense of democracy.

However, here's the liberating truth: Perceptions can change.

They have changed before. There was a time when kings ruled by divine right, and everyone perceived this as natural and inevitable. There was a time when slavery was perceived as the proper order of things. There was a time when the subordination of women was perceived as biological destiny. There was a time when the oceans were perceived as so vast that they could swallow all the pollution poured into them. There was a time when forests, plants, and animals were thought to be so infinite that they could withstand limitless destruction.

Those perceptions didn't just fade away. They were challenged, contested, and ultimately overthrown—by people who dared to see differently and helped others see differently too.

We can do this again.

CHANGING THE DREAM

During my work with Indigenous communities in the Amazon, I learned a phrase that has stayed with me: "Change the dream and you change the world." The title of a book I wrote long before the *Confessions* trilogy proclaims it: *The World Is As You Dream It.*

The Achuar and Shuar I've lived and worked with understand something profound. They see that the industrialized world is caught in a dream—a collective trance of materialism, extraction, and domination. This dream is demolishing the forests, poisoning the rivers, and destabilizing the climate. But it is also destroying those at the top of the hierarchy, leaving them isolated, anxious, and spiritually impoverished despite their material abundance.

My Indigenous friends don't tell us that the solution lies in new policies or new technologies. They say we need a new dream—a new way of perceiving ourselves, each other, and our relationship to the living Earth. They also say that if new policies and new technologies can help us do this, then we should adopt them.

This is not as abstract as it may sound. Every great transformation in human history began with a shift in perception.

The American Revolution started when colonists stopped perceiving themselves as British subjects and started perceiving themselves as free citizens of a new nation. George Washington's recollection of the defeat of a large British force in 1757 by a much smaller band of French and Indians at the Battle of the Monongahela generated the idea that "the British aren't invincible. All we have to do is hide behind trees." The perception preceded the reality—and then created it.

The civil rights movement took off when enough people stopped perceiving segregation as normal and recognized it as an abomination. The laws changed because the perception changed first.

The environmental movement began when people stopped perceiving nature as an infinite resource to be exploited and acknowledged that it is a finite, interconnected, fragile system that sustains all life.

In each case, changing the perception changed the actions. And changing the actions changed the reality.

THE DOMINANT PERCEPTIONS

The EHM strategy relies heavily on two dominant perceptions.

The first is that more is better. More money, more possessions, more power. This is the dream of extreme materialism. It has become a nightmare. It is killing us.

People are dying in wars fought over the desire for more resources and the actions that follow. Extraction, consumption, and pollution are killing the planet's forests, rivers, and oceans. In a similar fashion, inequality is shredding the social fabric of our communities. At the same time, increasing numbers of individuals are suffering from stress, anxiety, and the hollow dissatisfaction that comes from chasing a goal that recedes forever.

It is time to end the more-is-better obsession.

This is not a new insight. The Buddha taught that craving is the root of suffering. The ancient Greek and Roman Stoics argued that virtue, not wealth, produces human flourishing. Many North American Indigenous cultures traditionally measure wealth by what people give away, not by what they keep. The Tao Te Ching declares: "He who knows he has enough is rich." The prophets, saints, and texts of major religions reflect the words of Christ: "Blessed are the meek, for they shall inherit the earth." And the Shuar and Achuar shamans I've worked with for decades understand that community and reciprocity with *Pachamama*—Mother

Earth in their language—matter far more than accumulation. These are not cultures that lack the means to acquire. They are wisdom traditions that recognize what our culture seems to have forgotten: that the relentless pursuit of more often produces less—less time, less connection, less meaning in life.

What if we perceived success differently?

What if we defined success as strong relationships rather than large bank accounts? What if success meant contributing to community rather than accumulating for oneself? What if success meant leaving the world better than we found it, rather than extracting as much as possible before we die?

These aren't utopian fantasies. They're descriptions of how our ancestors lived for most of history—and how many still live today, in communities that haven't fully succumbed to the materialist dream. Changing this perception is not about sacrifice. It's about liberation. It's about escaping a treadmill that doesn't take us anywhere worth going.

The second dominant perception is that we must defer to power—to the "authorities."

We have been trained to look up to and admire the wealthy, to obey people who claim power, to assume that those at the top of hierarchies deserve to be there. This training starts early. Schools teach obedience. Workplaces demand compliance. The media celebrates billionaires and treats their pronouncements as intelligence. But democracy—and the Global Ideal—are founded on radically different perceptions. Power flows from the people. Authority must be earned and can be revoked. No one is inherently superior to anyone else.

These perceptions have been systematically undermined in the United States. *Citizens United* legalized money as speech, which means those with more money have more voice. Conservative lawmakers roll back voting rights and implement gerrymandering to send a message that politicians can choose their voters rather than voters choosing their representatives. Voter suppression sends a message that some people's participation matters less than others.

The economic hit men and the oligarchy they serve want us to perceive ourselves as spectators rather than participants. As subjects rather than citizens. As consumers rather than creators of systems that serve all of us. Changing these perceptions means reclaiming our sense of agency. It means understanding that the powerful are powerful only because the rest of us allow them to be. It means recognizing that systems that seem immovable were built by people and can be dismantled by people.

Every time someone says, "That's just how things are," that person is defending a perception that serves the oligarchy. Every time people ask, "What can one person do?" they are accepting a story designed to produce passivity. They are falling under the economic hit man spell.

The truth is different. One person who helps shift the perception of many people can change everything.

HOW TO CHANGE PERCEPTIONS

If perception is so powerful, how do we change it—in ourselves and in others?

This is not primarily an intellectual process. You cannot argue someone out of a perception they've absorbed through a lifetime of cultural immersion. Facts alone don't transform worldviews. If they did, wars would have ended and climate change would have been solved decades ago.

Perception changes through the following:

EXPERIENCE

Direct experience is a major factor in molding perceptions. When "once-in-a century" floods strike every year, people understand the destructive nature of climate change. When people get to know immigrants as neighbors and friends, fear-based narratives lose their power. When people experience genuine community, they recognize that the isolation of materialism is a form of impoverishment. This is why the EHM strategy works so hard to keep us separated—in segregated suburbs, in gated communities, in ideological bubbles, in patterns of life that minimize contact across differences.

Pointing out the true impacts of experience is important. "Those neighbors may speak with heavy accents, but they are extremely helpful and generous."

STORY

Humans understand the world through stories, and we change our understanding when we encounter new stories that ring true. The economic hit man system tells stories constantly: stories about the "deserving" and "hardworking" rich and the "undeserving" and "lazy" poor, about "dangerous" outsiders and autocrats who claim to "protect" us, about the "necessity" of hierarchy and the "folly" of the masses.

Counterstories—personal testimonies, historical memory, visions of alternative futures—are essential.

COMMUNITY

Perception is often a social construct. We see what the people around us see; we believe what our community believes. When communal perceptions change, so do communal realities. This is why movements are effective. And why autocrats suppress them.

REPETITION

The dominant perception did not take hold overnight. It was built through constant reinforcement—in advertising, entertainment, news, education, and political rhetoric. Trump understands this and constantly repeats whatever he wants Americans to believe. Shifting perceptions requires equally persistent countermessaging. Not propaganda, but truth-telling, repeated until it penetrates the fog of deception.

CRISIS

Sometimes perception shifts suddenly when reality becomes impossible to deny. The Great Depression changed perceptions of unregulated capitalism. The civil rights movement's images of violence against peaceful protesters changed perceptions of segregation. The climate crisis is creating openings for new perceptions of our relationship to nature. The videos of the ICE killings in Minnesota change perceptions around uncontrolled immigration enforcement.

The crises around Trump's economic hit man presidency can be perceived as a gift because they have shaken us awake to our need to change.

We cannot control all these factors. But we can influence many of them, starting with ourselves. When we do, we end the EHM strategy that has created a self-destructive, degenerative, and unsustainable Death Economy. Today, we have the opportunity to transform that into a regenerative, sustainable Life Economy.

And to manifest the Global Ideal.

Conclusion

What You Can Do

I BEGAN THIS BOOK by defining the four pillars of the EHM strategy—fear, debt, anxiety over insufficiency, and divide and conquer. In the chapters that followed, I explained how I was trained to use these tactics abroad, how they were deployed against economically vulnerable nations, how every president in my lifetime has employed them to enrich corporations and elites while hollowing out democracies, and how Trump has amplified them and adjusted them to fit his personality.

Trump did not need to invent a new system. He inherited one already perfected over decades—one that rewards those who understand how to manipulate perception, manufacture fear, and turn people against one another. Trump simply uses these tools openly, unapologetically, and for personal gain.

But, just as my earlier confessions were never only about me, this book is not about Trump alone. It is about a system that no longer serves the Global Ideal—principles rooted in liberty with responsibility, equality, justice, democracy, opportunity, and an individualism that supports family and community.

That system depends on our participation. Your participation.

And that means we can change it. You can change it.

The task may at first appear daunting. Yet systems are made of people, and three truths follow from that fact:

- Systems change when people change their perceptions.
- Systems have many entry points that cause structural change.
- There are numerous avenues to those entry points.

Each one of us can choose the entry point that suits us best. We each have our own unique personalities, interests, and abilities.

You don't have to fly to Minneapolis to support protesters there. You can write articles, make a TikTok video, or help neighbors understand the threat against all of us when masked, heavily armed agents invade a US city. You don't have to be an environmental expert to spread the word that the quality of water in your community will be impacted if a new business is allowed to dump toxins into a local river. You don't have to have a PhD in zoology to ask a book club to select a book on animal rights.

Whatever your background, you already have many resources. Actions like riding a bicycle, bringing your own shopping bags to the market, picking up litter, and planting a tree carry strong messages. In addition to the overt benefits, these seemingly small actions can inspire others to follow suit.

Consider these examples:

- **Rosa Parks** refused to give up her seat on a bus and accelerated the US civil rights movement.
- **Mohandas Gandhi** walked to the sea, picked up salt, and shattered the moral authority of British rule in India.
- **Malala Yousafzai** wrote a blog post about her life as a schoolgirl under the Taliban and spurred a global movement for girls' education, for which she won a Nobel Prize.
- **Greta Thunberg** sat alone with a hand-painted sign outside the Swedish parliament and inspired a worldwide climate movement.

- **Harriet Tubman** escaped slavery and sparked the liberation of hundreds of slaves.
- **Dietrich Bonhoeffer** preached sermons against Nazism and helped shape theological resistance to fascism across Europe.
- **Rachel Carson** wrote *Silent Spring,* and launched the modern environmental movement.
- **A small group of women in Iceland** took one day off from work and initiated a drive for gender equality that changed national policy.

These people had no idea when they started that they would be successful. They simply told the truth, refused to comply with the status quo, acted, and shared their stories. History often pivots not on grand gestures, but on *small acts.*

In the summer of 1777, the American army was in disarray. Soldiers lacked food, clothes, shoes, and ammunition. A massive British force marching from Canada toward New York City ravaged the countryside and took Fort Ticonderoga, a garrison that had been considered invincible. US soldiers were deserting in droves.

Then a woman named Jane McCrea, who was on her way to marry a British soldier, was killed and scalped by Indians loyal to the Crown. Someone had the idea that her murder should serve as a rallying cry. Others agreed. Riders fanned out across the countryside spreading the word that the English and their Indian allies were killing and scalping women and children—including those loyal to the British. No one was safe.

Colonists answered the call and rushed to the American army. Untrained, unpaid farmers, merchants, and teachers defeated the British at the Battle of Saratoga. It was a turning point in the war that also convinced the French to recognize the United States as a sovereign country. They sent money, ships, and soldiers—an alliance that was instrumental in winning the war.

All because someone had an idea and spoke up.

There are countless examples of the way one person can cause significant changes. I would not have written this book—or any book—had it not been for two teachers at Tilton School, my high school. A history teacher, Jack Woodbury, and an English teacher, Richard Davis, taught me that the pen is indeed mightier than the sword. Those two teachers changed my life.

When I was very young, my nana and I built a tower of blocks. She told me to pull one out near the bottom. The whole tower collapsed. "That's what you do if an obstacle seems too big," she told me. "Pull one part of it away, and you'll find the obstacle gets smaller, and collapses."

We each have a role to play in ending this reign of the oligarchs. Here is what you can do.

FIVE QUESTIONS

To start, ask yourself five questions:

1. What do I most want to do for the next few weeks, months, or years?

   It's important to recognize that only when we involve ourselves in tasks that bring us joy and satisfaction—when we follow our bliss—can we truly be successful. This may be the job you always wanted, or something you thought was unreachable. It may be a full-time or a part-time activity. Once you commit to doing it, you'll be surprised at the ways the universe helps you.

   Examples: For me, it is writing. I love to write. I have a friend who's a carpenter; for him, it's working with his hands and wood.

   Whether you like to work with words or wood, are a teacher or student, beginning a career or retiring, ask yourself this question and commit to honoring the answer. The only right answer is the one that inspires and fulfills YOU.

2. How can I do this in a way that will help manifest the Global Ideal? How can I help turn the Death Economy into a Life Economy?

   Examples: For me, it's writing to expose the problems and inspire actions that help solve them. For my carpenter friend, it's using sustainable wood and replanting a tree for every tree that is cut for his work.

3. What perceptions have blocked me or might block me in the future from doing these two things?

   Examples: For me, a blockage was believing that I wasn't educated enough to be a writer. For my carpenter friend, it was believing that his clients did not want to pay a little more for sustainable materials.

4. When I confront the blockages, rather than running from or denying them, how does that change my perception and allow me to act differently?

   Examples: For me, it was recognizing that Mark Twain, Maya Angelou, Ray Bradbury, William Faulkner, Jack London, J. K. Rowling, and many other successful writers were less educated than I was. For my carpenter friend, it was helping his clients understand that the extra price is not a cost; it is an investment in the future.

5. What actions do I take right now?

   Examples: For me, it's deciding what to write, and sitting down at my computer and writing for at least an hour a day, four days a week. For my carpenter friend, it's seeking out reclaimed lumber and rescuing old wood from landfills and derelict barns, as well as planting trees. It's important not to place the bar too high, especially at first. Make it fun.

> Don't overwhelm yourself. If you place the bar too high, you set yourself up for failure. Writing for an hour a day is a very attainable goal for me; as I get into that habit, I may find myself increasing to ninety minutes or two hours. And if I get bored with what I'm writing, I put it aside and start something else.

You may find that the answers to the first two questions remain the same for extended periods of time. However, the last three are likely to change frequently. For example, once I've decided what to write, I have to decide what voice to use—mine or that of a third person. Then, I have to decide how to begin. And so on . . .

Therefore, you may find it advantageous to review these questions often. After a little practice, you'll be able to do it in just a few minutes, perhaps while lying in bed right after waking up. Each time, it gets easier and more creative and fun.

THE DALAI LAMA'S ADVICE

On a flight from Leh, Ladakh, to Jammu, India, the group I was leading ended up on the same plane as the Dalai Lama. When he learned that I was the author of a book he was reading (*Shapeshifting*) about Indigenous cultures, he invited me to sit next to him. We had a lively discussion about shamanism. When the plane landed, he invited my group to visit him at his house in Dharamsala.

As we chatted during that meeting, he told us that it is good to pray for peace. "But," he added, "if that is all you do, it's a waste of time. It may even be a distraction. You need to take appropriate daily action." He smiled. "You must act. Every day."

The Dalai Lama is a great example of a person who meditates, explores perceptions, and then acts. He writes books, gives speeches around the world, and encourages people from all stations in life to act to create a more compassionate and sustainable world.

What follows are some ideas that may help you answer the five questions. Don't expect to relate to all of them. Just one may appeal to you, or you may have some other approach that works better. The important thing is to do what you most want to do and do it in a conscious way to end the EHM strategy and the oppressive, degenerative system that it creates. Contribute to manifesting the Global Ideal of liberty with responsibility, equality, justice, democracy, opportunity, and an individualism that supports family and community.

CHANGE YOUR OWN PERCEPTIONS

The economic hit man system depends on your participation. And that means it can be changed. Fear only works if you believe the threat is real and truly dangerous. Debt only works if you believe your value depends on constant materialistic growth or owing favors to others. Anxiety over insufficiency only works if you believe there is never enough. Divisiveness only works if you believe someone else is the problem.

These beliefs are not facts. They are narratives—carefully cultivated, endlessly repeated, and rarely questioned. **Changing perceptions** is a radical act. When we stop seeing the world as a zero-sum contest and begin recognizing it as an interdependent system, our actions change. When our actions change, reality changes.

You might want to change some perceptions you've absorbed about:

SUCCESS

Do you measure your life by accumulation? By status? By comparison to others? What would it mean to measure it instead by contribution, relationship, integrity, and happiness?

POWER

Do you defer automatically to wealth and authority? Do you assume the system is too big to challenge? What would it mean to see yourself as a person with agency rather than a subject without power?

OTHERS

Have you accepted the divisions the system promotes? Do you see certain groups as threats, as competitors, as less-than? What would it mean to see them as potential allies in a shared struggle?

POSSIBILITY

Do you believe the future is fixed? That the way things are is the way they must be? What would it mean to perceive history as open, as shaped by human choices, including yours?

These questions aren't self-help platitudes. They are about recognizing that the system's power depends partly on our internalization of its premises. Every perception you change in yourself is one less foothold for the oligarchy.

REFUSE THE FOUR PILLARS

Once you see the pillars clearly, you can refuse them.

Fear

Step beyond fear. Fear of the "other." Fear of falling behind. Fear of speaking out. Fear of failure. Fear of success.

Fear is the economic hit man's currency. It keeps people obedient. It narrows imagination. It justifies cruelty. Refusing fear does not mean ignoring danger. It means refusing to let fear govern your decisions.

When leaders ask you to fear immigrants, neighbors, other nations, or people who look or think differently, ask: "Who benefits from this fear? What am I actually afraid of? How much of that fear has been manufactured by the media, politicians, and advertisers who profit from my anxiety?" Fear empowers the oligarchy.

Courage—especially quiet, everyday courage—weakens the architecture of control more effectively than outrage.

Fear is useful when it alerts us to genuine danger. It is weaponized when it keeps us frozen, compliant, or hostile to people who should be our allies. Like all emotions, fear expresses itself as energy. The important thing is to use that energy to create positive change, not to fall under the spell of someone who promises to pull you out of whatever it is you fear. Don't simply run away from that which you fear. Run toward what you want. Courage is not about lacking fear; it's about using fear to energize positive actions.

Debt

Break the chains of debt.

Of all the pillars of the EHM strategy, debt is the most deceptive. Fear shouts. Division sidetracks. Scarcity distracts. Debt is the quiet chain that enslaves; it whispers.

I learned early in my career that debt is not merely a financial instrument. It is a psychological one. A nation in debt behaves differently. It lowers its voice. It narrows its options. It trades sovereignty for the hope of relief. It learns to comply. Debt does not need soldiers. It does not need coups. What makes debt so powerful is that it masquerades as responsibility. We are taught that usury is okay and that failure to repay exploitative interest rates is a moral sin. The economic hit man system manipulates this deeply ingrained belief. It turns obligation into guilt and obedience.

When countries fell into debt, I watched leaders abandon long-term visions for short-term survival. Schools went unfunded. Hospitals closed. Environmental and social protections vanished. Everything not immediately profitable was sacrificed to service the debt.

The same logic now governs American life. Student debt ends dreams. Medical debt turns illness into lifelong punishment. Mortgage debt chains people to jobs they hate and communities they cannot leave. Credit card debt enslaves people, encouraging them to purchase goods they cannot afford and do not really need. National debt becomes a justification for cutting social programs while protecting corporate privilege.

Debt narrows imagination. It convinces people that "there is no alternative." That the future has already been mortgaged. That survival requires submission. This is not an accident. It is the strategy.

Economic hit men do not need to collect the full debt. In fact, they rarely want to. A debt that can be repaid loses its leverage. A debt that lingers—just manageable enough to avoid revolt, just crushing enough to prevent resistance—is ideal. It creates dependency and surrenders control.

For individuals, debt personalizes blame. It teaches people to see systemic exploitation as personal failure. When that happens, anger turns inward instead of upward. The system remains intact. Breaking this pillar does not begin with default or revolution. It begins with reframing. Debt is not a measure of worth. It is a tool that can be challenged, renegotiated, forgiven, and reimagined. When people understand this, something remarkable happens. Shame dissolves. Fear loosens. Collective solutions become thinkable again.

When you hear that the United States, the World Bank, or one of the other big financial institutions is "giving" money to a country, ask whether this is a grant or a loan and, if it is a loan, what are the terms, interest rates, buyback period, collateral, and conditionalities.

If you are in debt yourself or considering it, know that it can be an enslaving chain. It may tie you to a job you hate, a house you'd rather leave, choices that serve creditors rather than you. Be aware of the terms and conditions and of alternatives. Avoid stumbling into the debt trap.

And remember, debt is not just about money. Don't fall into the debt trap of owing people favors—or perceived favors. Don't become part of the "Godfather syndrome," where a Don Corleone lures you into a transactional relationship. Do not allow someone or some institution to intimidate you through the psychology of personal loyalty debt. It is predatory lending applied to human relationships.

Anxiety over Insufficiency

Break the spell of anxiety over insufficiency.

Scarcity is not merely economic. It is emotional and psychological. It persists because it is profitable. We are told there is not enough time, security, opportunity, or compassion—in addition to money.

Economic hit men thrive in cultures that equate success with accumulation. More money. More power. More dominance. But the Global Ideal was never about materialistic hoarding. It is about possibility—the possibility to live with dignity, purpose, connection, and opportunity.

As examples in this book have shown, one of my most important jobs in many nations was to convince the leaders that they lived in poor countries little better than ones during medieval times. The yardsticks I advocated measured prosperity as we defined it.

But, as I discovered when I lived among the Shuar during my Peace Corps days, this can be a lie. All the reports and statistics I'd seen classified them as below the poverty line. However, what I found were people who had everything they needed, including a joyous sense of community and close-knit, loving families.

This is not to negate the desperation that comes from real scarcity of things that are essential to life—food, clothing, shelter, compassion. Life-threatening scarcity exists for billions of people, and it is horrible and unjustifiable. It is an abomination of the economic hit man system. It does not need to happen in a world with so many resources—and a handful (relatively speaking) of greedy, selfish oligarchs.

Africa is the wealthiest continent in the world from a resource standpoint and the poorest from a human prosperity standpoint. That is a terrible comment on the way our economic system has been institutionalized to favor the rich and powerful, the exploiters, over those who are forced to live without basic life support systems.

For many of us, the perception of insufficiency drives us to accumulate beyond need, to hoard rather than share, to see neighbors as competitors for limited resources. It is important to recognize that much of this scarcity is manufactured. There is enough—enough food, enough shelter, enough possibility—if we refuse systems designed to concentrate abundance in a few hands.

In your life, choose generosity of time, resources, listening, and caring. Not as charity, but as a gift to yourself and others. Generosity undermines the myth that we must compete to survive.

Ask yourself:

- Does my work contribute to life or merely extract from it?
- Does my consumption strengthen community or weaken it?
- Do my investments align with my values or contradict them?
- Have I been tricked into false beliefs around scarcity?

You do not need to reject prosperity. You may simply need to redefine it.

Divide and Conquer

This pillar needs little explanation. It speaks for itself. For each of us—for you—it is important simply to refuse to be divided.

Don't be swayed by propaganda that categorizes people in ways that generalize and try to turn us against our neighbors.

This was highlighted in December 2025 when a video posted on YouTube just after Christmas by a right-wing content creator went viral. It claimed that childcare centers in Minnesota operated by Somali Americans were fraudulent "ghost" centers with no children present. As a result, Trump temporarily froze federal childcare funds to all fifty states.

The video generated threats and harassment against Somalis and daycare providers in general. Subsequent propaganda resulted in vandalism, a climate of fear and economic instability within the Somali community, increasing anti-immigrant sentiment, and hardship for parents who were left with nowhere to leave their children while they were at work. The video has since been debunked by investigators as inaccurate and misleading.[51] But, whether the video was true or not, the fallout had a hugely negative effect in classifying two groups of people—Somali immigrants and daycare providers—as problematic and dangerous. This is just one example of how propaganda can militarize divisions within the American public.

Divide and conquer works only when we accept false binaries. Red versus blue. Us versus them. Winners versus losers.

Who benefits when you fight with your neighbor? When you see immigrants, or rural Americans, or city dwellers, or people of different faiths or races or countries as enemies? Every moment you spend in conflict with people who share your basic needs and fundamental rights is a moment you're not challenging the structures that exploit you both.

Know that you do not have to agree with people to recognize their humanity. You do not have to share ideology to share a future. Look for common ground in things you desire: safe communities, meaningful work, healthy children, clean air and water, dignity in aging.

These are not partisan values. They are human values.

FOLLOW THE MONEY—YOUR MONEY

Use your economic power consciously. Every dollar you spend is a vote. Every investment, every bank account, every subscription is an endorsement. The oligarchy consolidates power through corporate control. Your dollars either feed that consolidation or starve it. Every purchase is a choice about which systems to support.

Economic hit men depend on passive participation. Conscious participation disrupts them. You cannot disengage completely, but you can engage consciously. Support local businesses. Favor cooperatives and employee-owned firms. Invest in renewable energy and regenerative practices—at home and in the marketplace. Pressure corporations through your consumer and investment choices.

It may seem like a cliché, but it's a fact: You vote with your wallet.

This doesn't mean you can shop your way to revolution. It does mean paying attention:

- Where is your money held? Big banks fund pipelines, private prisons, and political campaigns that undermine democracy. Credit unions and community banks keep capital local.
- What do you buy? From whom? Supply chains are long and often hidden. But information is more accessible than ever. Companies that exploit workers, devastate environments, and corrupt politicians depend on consumer ignorance.
- If you invest, what do you support? Retirement accounts and many mutual funds are likely to invest in the very corporations whose practices you oppose. Socially responsible investment options exist. They're not perfect, but they're better than the ones that ignore environmental and social impacts.

Money is the language the system speaks. Learn the vocabulary, and speak it consciously.

BUILD LOCAL POWER

Strengthen democracy where you live.

Democracy is not something that happens just in Washington. It happens in neighborhoods, schools, workplaces, and town halls. It happens when you show up, listen, speak up, vote, organize, or serve.

Strong communities are the greatest threat to economic hit man systems. National politics capture our attention, but local politics shape our lives. Your school board decides what children learn—including what perceptions they absorb. Your city council determines housing policy, police practices, zoning laws. Your state legislature draws district lines, regulates businesses, allocates resources. These are the arenas where engaged citizens can make immediate, tangible differences.

The oligarchy understands this. That's why dark money has begun flooding into local races, why partisan think tanks now groom candidates for school boards and county commissions, and why voter suppression efforts now target municipal elections.

Support local journalism. Democracy dies in darkness, and the darkness is thickest at the local level, where newspapers have collapsed and no one covers the county budget. Write letters and op-eds. Produce your own newsletter, podcast, TikTok discussion group, or YouTube channel. Run for office, or recruit or support someone you trust. The pipeline of candidates for higher office starts at the local level. If good people don't enter that pipeline, only bad ones will emerge from it.

SUPPORT OPPORTUNITY AND SOLIDARITY

Supporting causes that help people "learn to fish" rather than "giving them a fish" creates real opportunities for individual progress. While charity may be appropriate for those who have no way at all to help themselves, it often undermines true progress and maintains the system. Teaching people skills that enable them to help themselves provides dignity and creates solidarity in society. Donating money to political candidates; NGOs that protect the environment, civil liberties, and social rights; and other such causes is not charity, but a form of supporting causes we believe in. Solidarity challenges the system. Unqualified charity fosters the perception that inequality is natural.

Today, solidarity means:

- Supporting campaigns that demand that top executives not be paid millions—or billions—of dollars while workers are denied a livable wage, health care, or retirement funds
- Standing with communities facing environmental destruction and racism, even if the pollution or bigotry isn't in your backyard
- Defending immigrants' rights, even if your own family has been here for generations
- Protecting voter rights, especially for those whose votes are most suppressed

Your interests are bound up with those of your neighbor—and when you come down to the truth of the modern world, everybody is your neighbor. The system that exploits them is exploiting you too. Solidarity is not altruism. It is survival.

TELL DIFFERENT STORIES

The economic hit man system depends on manufactured consent—on narratives that justify extraction and exploitation, that normalize inequality and obscure the mechanics of power.

A counternarrative is resistance.

Tell your own story. How has the system affected your life, your family, your community? Personal testimony cuts through abstraction and shifts perception in ways that statistics cannot. Share what you learn. Many people have no idea how the economy actually works, how wealth is concentrated, how political power is purchased. Change requires information.

Offer alternative visions. It's not enough to criticize the existing perceptions; we need to articulate better ones. What does a society look like that measures success by well-being rather than GDP?

That values adequacy over accumulation? That practices democracy from the ground up?

Here are some options:

- Participate in conversations in groups at libraries, bookstores, churches, and book clubs—or create one of your own.
- If you are a writer, playwright, actor, musician, dancer, teacher, painter, or parent, use that position to tell your story and inspire people to join you in defying systems that are failing us.
- Create a YouTube channel, a TikTok discussion group, or another social networking channel.
- Speak up at town hall or city council meetings. Make it personal. When you tell your own story and combine it with a larger issue, it appeals to listeners' emotions, helps them move to new perceptions, and encourages them to take the actions that generate change.
- Be creative. Come up with your own ideas about getting stories across that expose policies, actions, and systems that are failing us—and suggest better ones.

AVOID BURNOUT

Resistance is exhausting. The system counts on you being worn out and worn down.

Burnout serves power. When activists collapse, movements falter. When citizens disengage because of despair, oligarchs win by default. Personal, emotional sustainability isn't a luxury; it's a strategic necessity.

Protect your emotional health. Constant outrage is not sustainable. Neither is constant consumption of catastrophic news. Stay informed, but set boundaries. The system benefits when you're too anxious, exhausted, or overwhelmed to function.

Model the alternative. The most powerful way to shift perception is to embody an enthusiastic way of being. When people encounter someone who has genuinely escaped the trance of materialism, deference, and despair—someone who lives with sufficiency, agency, and joy—it opens a window. It makes another world visible.

THIS TIME IN HISTORY

There are many ways to end the economic hit man system and the economic hit man presidency. This chapter has offered suggestions. They are meant as guideposts that may help you along the path to the Global Ideal. Answering the five questions has assisted me and many others. I encourage you to give it a try. However, above all, do whatever it is that most appeals to you. Act in ways that bring you satisfaction and open your heart to joy.

You and I are blessed to live at this time in history. Given all the events of the recent years—political, economic, social, environmental, and technological—we know we are at an inflection point. We are living at a moment when we are asked to redefine what it means to be successful human beings being human on this beautiful planet. We are living at a time that echoes a moment two hundred and fifty years ago when, in 1776, Thomas Paine wrote:

> *These are the times that try men's souls. The summer soldier and the sunshine patriot will, in this crisis, shrink from the service of their country; but he that stands by it now, deserves the love and thanks of man and woman. Tyranny, like hell, is not easily conquered; yet we have this consolation with us, that the harder the conflict, the more glorious the triumph.*

Afterword

A Personal Note

THE ECONOMIC HIT MAN SYSTEM is powerful. It has captured governments, corporations, media, and the courts. It has shaped the perceptions of hundreds of millions of people. It has brought us to the edge of ecological catastrophe and political collapse.

But it is not invincible. Or inevitable.

Most harmful systems that seem permanent eventually fall. Monarchy. Feudalism. Slavery. Soviet Communism. Hitler's Nazism. The forces that sustained them seemed insurmountable—until they weren't. And in every case, the collapse was preceded by a shift in perception. People stopped believing in the system's legitimacy. They started perceiving alternatives as possible. Then they acted.

The publication of the *Confessions of an Economic Hit Man* trilogy has given me the opportunity to travel around the world. I have spoken to and with people from many different cultures and walks of life, and countless numbers of them want to participate in global systemic change. They want to manifest the Global Ideal.

That Ideal has never been realized. But it has never been abandoned, either. In every generation, people have fought to narrow the gap between principle and practice. Our ancestors faced grave challenges, perhaps even graver than ours today. There were defeats. But there were enough victories to keep them—and us—marching toward the Ideal.

You and I are the inheritors of that struggle. We are alive at this moment because we have a mission. Thomas Paine challenged the people of his time to end the tyranny of the British monarchy and to march forward to a glorious triumph. Now it is our time to march forward. It is time to leave behind the dark shadows of an economic hit man presidency. It is time to march along the path lit by the Statue of Liberty's torch, a path that leads to the realization of the American Ideal—the Global Ideal.

The Art of the Steal

Discussion Guide

1. In general, what do economic hit men do to debt-trap a country and gain access to its resources?
2. What did Trump do in January 2026 that defined the nature of his economic hit man presidency? How did he justify each of his actions?
3. Perkins claims that he believed in what he was doing as an economic hit man during the majority of his years in that career. Do you believe him? Why or why not?
4. How is the economic hit man model adapted to countries, such as Iran and Saudi Arabia, that don't need loans?
5. What does Perkins say about the relationship between perceptions and reality? Do you agree with him? Why or why not?
6. How do metrics like gross domestic product (GDP) contribute to the EHM strategy?
7. Perkins describes the three distinctive waves—eras—in the evolution of the economic hit men and their strategy. What are they? How do they differ from each other?

8. If you were the leader of a country with natural resources coveted by both the United States and China, and your country did not have the technology to exploit those resources, what would you do?
9. Do you believe that China is overtaking the United States as a world leader? What evidence does Perkins provide for this assertion? What else can you think of to confirm or reject it?
10. Provide at least two examples of the way economic hit men have applied the pillar of fear in other countries, then compare and contrast these with actions taken by Trump.
11. How has Trump used the pillar of debt that does not involve monetary debt?
12. How has Trump transformed the traditional use of debt into a system that prevents the creditor from coming after him when he doesn't honor his obligations?
13. Do you think anxiety over insufficiency is a factor in people's lives in the country where you live? Does it impact you personally?
14. Perkins claims that the military actions against the president of Venezuela had much broader implications. Do you agree? Why or why not?
15. Were you aware of the US involvement in Operation Condor and of Argentina's role? How do you feel about that operation?
16. Do you agree with Perkins's definition of the American Ideal? Is it really a Global Ideal?
17. When you ask yourself and answer the five questions Perkins poses, do you feel empowered to move forward with your mission?

18. Perkins makes a number of suggestions to help readers answer the five questions. Which ones most appeal to you? Why?

19. How has this book impacted you? Be specific.

20. Do you think the Thomas Paine quote at the end of the book is relevant to our situation today?

Acknowledgments

I owe my deepest gratitude to my partner, Kiman Lucas. She has read, critiqued, and suggested changes to this and other manuscripts; edited my weekly newsletters; coached me before I gave speeches and interviews; organized and accompanied me on trips across the globe; and brought joy to my life.

My thanks to my daughter, Jessica Perkins, who inspires me with her success as a local community organizer and is always there when I need her; to her husband and my son-in-law, Derek Stabelfeldt, who supplies me with a stream of important books and engages me in stimulating discussions; and to my ex-wife, Winifred Grant Perkins, who over so many years has supported me in countless ways.

I am eternally grateful to my grandson Grant Miller, who gives me hope for the future, challenges me to think outside the box, and who took time off from his busy senior year in high school to join and assist me in the Amazon. On top of everything else he has done for me and so many others, he was a great help to the documentary film crew that accompanied us while I was writing this book in January 2026.

Speaking of that, I am grateful to filmmaker John Lopez; his producer, Pete La Raus; their cameraman, Rubén Collado; and the nine other people they assembled for that trip deep into the Ecuadorian rainforest. John has devoted immeasurable hours and creative energy over the past three years to making an amazing film about the EHM strategy and my role in it. He is a great example of using film as a medium for changing the world.

I owe an especially big thanks to my friend David Korten, author of many important books and articles, including *When Corporations Rule the World, The Great Turning*, and *Change the Story, Change the Future.* During our weekly lunch meetings, David has offered brilliant insights and urged me to keep writing.

And where would I be were it not for my friend and teacher Daniel Koupermann? He made it possible for me to reconnect with the Shuar and Achuar back in the 1980s. Without him there would be no Dream Change or Pachamama Alliance. Thank you, Daniel.

And thank you, Bill and Lynne Twist, for answering the call and devoting thirty years of your lives to the Pachamama Alliance and changing the dream of the modern world.

A special thanks to Paige Harbour and Killian Lucas, who continue to guide me through the maze of modern technology and AI. They have been essential to spreading the word of this and past books through their social networking skills.

I thank Berrett-Koehler founder and publisher, Steve Piersanti, and vice president of editorial, Jeevan Sivasubramaniam, who came up with the idea for this book at the same time I did, encouraged me to write it, and have supported me for the past twenty years as they published my previous four BK books. Thanks to Tai Moses, who did a magnificent job of editing and commenting on the original draft of the manuscript; Rachel Monaghan, who was brilliant once again in helping me craft the book, Maureen Forys, book producer, who skillfully managed the production of the book; and Christy Kirk for all her support in promoting the book.

A special thanks to the people at Berrett-Koehler, a great publisher: design and production team Ashley Ingram, Katelyn Keating, and Edward Wade; sales and marketing team Kristen Frantz, Catherine Lengronne, Sarah Nelson, Elsa Frantz, and Trenae Williams; and editorial team (in addition to Steve and Jeevan) Alexis Woodcock and Neal Maillet.

I also want to thank the people who shared experiences with me over the years and are mentioned in this book. Whenever I re-create conversations with them, I rely on personal records, recollections, and notes I took at the time. Their contributions to this book are beyond measure.

Notes

1. Trump demands loyalty.

LOYALTY OVER LAW

- Northwestern University research by political scientist Daniel Galvin documents Trump's party domination efforts, including stifling dissent, bullying opponents, and demanding loyalty. Daniel Galvin, "Examining President Trump's Unusual Style of Party Leadership," Institute for Policy Research, Northwestern University, August 13, 2020.
- Personality assessment research published by Saint John's University found that Trump has a predilection for personal connections and loyalty over competence in his staffing decisions and appointments. Aubrey Immelman, "The Leadership Style of U.S. President Donald J. Trump," DigitalCommons@CSB/SJU, Psychology Faculty Publications, College of Saint Benedict and Saint John's University, January 20, 2017, https://digitalcommons.csbsju.edu/cgi/viewcontent.cgi?article=1109&context=psychology_pubs.
- *The Fulcrum* reported that Trump told then-FBI Director James Comey early in his first term: "I need loyalty; I expect loyalty." Austin Sarat, "Loyalty, Democracy, and the

Future of American Politics," *The Fulcrum*, February 4, 2025, https://thefulcrum.us/ethics-leadership/donald-trump-and-loyalty.

- *Focus Insight* notes that Trump created an atmosphere of personal loyalty over institutional integrity, often demanding that officials show unwavering loyalty and dismissing several high-profile figures when they failed to meet this expectation. "Donald Trump's Leadership Style: A Comprehensive Analysis," *Focus Insight*, https://focusinsight.net/donald-trumps-leadership-style.

AGGRESSIVE NATIONALISM AND PUBLIC THREATS

- CNN documented Trump's statement regarding Greenland ("We need Greenland from the standpoint of national security") and his threats toward multiple countries. Tim Lister, "From Greenland to Iran: Trump's Threats Stretch Far and Wide Since His Venezuela Strike," CNN, January 6, 2026, https://www.cnn.com/2026/01/05/world/greenland-cuba-iran-trump-warning-intl.
- *Axios* compiled a list showing Trump threatened eleven countries, including military action in Colombia and Venezuela, and territorial claims on Greenland and the Panama Canal. Herb Scribner, "Mapped: The Countries Trump Is Threatening—and Why," *Axios*, January 7, 2026, https://www.axios.com/2026/01/07/trump-venezuela-greenland-countries-threats.
- *Foreign Affairs* described Trump's approach through advisor Stephen Miller's statement that "we live in a world, in the real world . . . that is governed by strength, that is governed by force, that is governed by power." Michael Singh, "America the Fearful: Visions of Decline Are a Self-Fulfilling Prophecy," *Foreign Affairs*, February 11, 2026, https://www.foreignaffairs.com/united-states/america-fearful.
- Wikipedia's analysis notes that Trump's rhetoric employs threats, xenophobia, national security scares, and inflammatory language, particularly when discussing immigration,

crime, and political adversaries. Wikipedia, "Rhetoric of Donald Trump," last modified March 13, 2026, 22:19 (UTC), https://en.wikipedia.org/wiki/Rhetoric_of_Donald_Trump.

WITHDRAWAL FROM MULTILATERAL AGREEMENTS

- The Council on Foreign Relations documented that Trump questioned the merits of US involvement in NATO, withdrew from the WHO and Paris Agreement, and implemented sweeping tariffs on foreign goods. Council on Foreign Relations, "U.S. Foreign Policy: Multilateralism or Unilateralism?," CFR Education, March 19, 2025, https://education.cfr.org/teach/mini-simulation/us-foreign-policy-multilateralism-or-unilateralism.
- The Miller Center states that a cornerstone of Trump's America First policy was the abrogation of bilateral and multilateral agreements in favor of unilateral arrangements conducted country to country. Benjamin C. Waterhouse, "Donald Trump: Foreign Affairs," Miller Center, University of Virginia, https://millercenter.org/president/trump/foreign-affairs.
- *Foreign Policy* reported that Trump announced his intent to withdraw the United States from sixty-six separate multilateral forums, retracted billions in spending for international organizations, and pulled back from the UN, WHO, UNESCO, and more. Suzanne Nossel, "The World Minus One Will Be a Mess: Multilateral Cooperation Will Struggle to Survive in Washington's Absence," *Foreign Policy*, January 14, 2026, https://foreignpolicy.com/2026/01/14/world-minus-one-trump-multilateralism-united-nations-treaties/.
- Analysis from the Brookings Institution concluded that the real driving force of Trump's trade policy boiled down to the pursuit of unilateralism: ensuring the United States enjoys wide berth in reinstating tariffs and weakening dispute settlement mechanisms. Mireya Solis, "'America First' Is a Losing Strategy on Trade," Brookings Institution, October 24, 2017, https://www.brookings.edu/articles/america-first-is-a-losing-strategy-on-trade/.

2. CNN reported Trump's statement aboard Air Force One: "We need Greenland. . . . It's so strategic right now. Greenland is covered with Russian and Chinese ships all over the place. We need Greenland from the standpoint of national security, and Denmark is not going to be able to do it." Tim Lister, "From Greenland to Iran: Trump's Threats Stretch Far and Wide Since His Venezuela Strike," CNN, January 6, 2026, https://www.cnn.com/2026/01/05/world/greenland-cuba-iran-trump-warning-intl.

3. Is Trump a buffoon or merely cunning?

ACADEMIC RESEARCH ON "BUFFOON" AS STRATEGIC POSITION

- *ScienceDirect* published research analyzing how Trump's opponents viewed him as a buffoon or a candidate who would soon implode or self-destruct, leading them to leave "The Donald" alone and use precious airtime to attack other mainstream candidates. The study found this strategic miscalculation actually enhanced his probability of winning. Micael Castanheira et al., "How Trump Triumphed: Multi-Candidate Primaries with Buffoons," *European Economic Review* 157 (August 2023), https://www.sciencedirect.com/science/article/abs/pii/S0014292123001356.

THEATRICS AS PERFORMANCE STRATEGY

- *Independent Australia* analyzed whether there's a method to Trump's madness, noting his governance style isn't about careful policy but about performance, creating an endless loop of crises, outrages, and headlines that forces media to cover him obsessively. Vince Hooper, "Strategic Mastermind or Agent of Chaos: The Method in Trump's Madness," *Independent Australia*, March 25, 2025, https://independentaustralia.net/politics/politics-display/strategic-mastermind-or-agent-of-chaos-the-method-in-trumps-madness,19566.
- Wikipedia on Trump's rhetoric notes that political theorist William E. Connolly compared Trump's integration of

theatrics and crowd participation with rhetoric involving grandiose bodily gestures, grimaces, hysterical charges, and dramatic repetitions. Wikipedia, "Rhetoric of Donald Trump," last modified March 13, 2026, 22:19 (UTC), https://en.wikipedia.org/wiki/Rhetoric_of_Donald_Trump.

- *TIME* magazine described how the Trump Doctrine involves American power as a lever deployed at will, subject to change at his whim, with world leaders increasingly treating the management of Trump's emotions as a strategic priority. Brian Bennett and Nik Popli, "How Trump's Foreign Policy Gambits Are Reshaping the World," *TIME*, January 15, 2026, https://time.com/collections/davos-2026/7345543/trump-foreign-policy-second-term/.

CHAOS AS CALCULATED STRATEGY

- *Medium* analysis argued that behind the apparent chaos of Trump's tariff policy lay a deliberate and structured strategy, with chaos not being a tactical error but a structured move to maximize negotiating power by shifting the rules of the game. Sergio Gevatschnaider, "Trump and Game Theory: Chaos as a Calculated Move: A Strategic Look at U.S. Tariff Policy Under Trump, Modeled as a Sequential Game with Credible Threats and Calculated Outcomes," *Medium*, April 7, 2025, https://medium.com/@sergiosear/trump-and-game-theory-chaos-as-a-calculated-move-21c6de8a34a2.
- The *Duke Chronicle* described Trump as a masterful manipulator of public perception rather than a "loose cannon," orchestrating crisis, controlling narratives, and feigning heroism for the sole purpose of garnering public approval. Aria Dwoskin, "Trump's Strategy of Manufactured Crisis: The TikTok Ban and Beyond," *The Chronicle*, Duke University, February 2, 2025, https://www.dukechronicle.com/article/2025/02/trump-manufactured-crisis-tiktok.

4. Immigrants favor the United States over China by far.

UNITED STATES IMMIGRATION

- Pew Research Center reported that as of June 2025, 51.9 million immigrants lived in the United States, making up 15.4 percent of the nation's population, with more than 40 million people living in the United States born in another country, accounting for about one-fifth of the world's migrants. Stephanie Kramer and Jeffrey S. Passel, "What the Data Says About Immigrants in the U.S.," Pew Research Center, August 21, 2025, https://www.pewresearch.org/short-reads/2025/08/21/key-findings-about-us-immigrants/.
- World Population Review noted that the United States has the highest immigrant population in the world at 50.6 million (as of mid-2020), which equates to approximately 15.3 percent of the total US population and 18 percent of international immigrants worldwide. World Population Review, "US Immigration by Country 2026," n.d., https://worldpopulationreview.com/country-rankings/us-immigration-by-country.

CHINA IMMIGRATION IS FAR LOWER

- In stark contrast, Wikipedia documented that according to the 2020 Chinese census, China has 1,430,695 immigrants, split between 845,697 foreign nationals and 584,998 residents of Hong Kong, Macao, and Taiwan. As of 2023, there are around 12,000 foreigners with permanent residency in China. Wikipedia, "Immigration to China," December 11, 2025, 02:11 (UTC), https://en.wikipedia.org/wiki/Immigration_to_China.
- The total number of immigrants in China amounted to just 0.1 percent of China's population of more than 1.41 billion people. This is exceptionally low not only compared to Western countries, such as the United States (15.4 percent), Germany (15.7 percent), and France (12.8 percent), but also compared to China's East Asian neighbors Japan (2.0 percent) and South Korea (2.3 percent). Frank Bickenbach and Wan-Hsin Liu, "Goodbye China: What Do Fewer Foreigners Mean

for Multinationals and the Chinese Economy?," *Intereconomics* 57, no. 5 (2022): 306–312, https://www.intereconomics.eu/contents/year/2022/number/5/article/goodbye-china-what-do-fewer-foreigners-mean-for-multinationals-and-the-chinese-economy.html.

THE SCALE OF THE DIFFERENCE

- To put this in perspective, the United States has approximately 50 million immigrants compared to China's less than 1.5 million, despite China having more than four times the population of the United States. The United States accepts more than thirty-five times as many immigrants despite having a much smaller population. This makes the United States by far the more preferred destination for international migrants globally.

5. Trump's goal is to build his family's net worth.

CRYPTOCURRENCY VENTURES

- According to multiple sources, World Liberty Financial (WLFI) has been the Trump family's most lucrative venture. The Trump family receives 75 percent of net proceeds when WLFI sells tokens, and gets a cut of stablecoin profits. By December 2025, the Trumps had profited $1 billion on proceeds, while holding $3 billion worth of unsold tokens. Wikipedia, "World Liberty Financial," last modified March 14, 2026, 07:15 (UTC), https://en.wikipedia.org/wiki/World_Liberty_Financial.
- ABC News reported that when WLFI's token began trading, the Trump family secured a roughly $5 billion windfall based on public disclosures reporting that "certain family members of Donald J. Trump [hold] 22.5 billion $WLFI tokens." Lucien Bruggeman, "Trump Family Profits from Launch of World Liberty Financial Crypto Token," ABC News, September 2, 2025, https://abcnews.com/US/trump-family-profits-launch-world-liberty-financial-crypto/story?id=125179318.

- House Judiciary Committee Democrats released a report finding that President Trump and his family have earned hundreds of millions of dollars and added billions to their net worth through a network of cryptocurrency ventures launched during and after his 2024 campaign, with crypto holdings worth as much as $11.6 billion and income of more than $800 million from the sale of crypto assets in the first half of 2025 alone. House Judiciary Committee Democrats, "Trump, Crypto, and a New Age of Corruption," November 25, 2025, https://democrats-judiciary.house.gov/sites/evo-subsites/democrats-judiciary.house.gov/files/evo-media-document/2025-11-24.hjc-dem-staff-report-trump-crypto-corruption-small_0.pdf.
- *Newsweek* reported that the Trump Organization earned $802 million from crypto during the first half of 2025, overtaking the family's income from traditional businesses like real estate and licensing deals, which only made up $62 million in the same period. Suzanne Blake, "Here's How Much Donald Trump Is Earning from Crypto During Presidency," *Newsweek*, October 29, 2025, https://www.newsweek.com/how-much-donald-trump-earning-crypto-during-presidency-10959978.

FOREIGN INVESTMENTS

- Wikipedia documented that in May 2025, MGX, an Abu Dhabi–state–backed company led by Tahnoun bin Zayed Al Nahyan of the Abu Dhabi royal family, announced it would use $2 billion worth of the USD1 stablecoin launched by World Liberty to finance a deal in crypto exchange Binance. Wikipedia, "World Liberty Financial," last modified March 14, 2026, 07:15 (UTC), https://en.wikipedia.org/wiki/World_Liberty_Financial.
- PBS reported that the Trump family crypto business just got a major $2 billion infusion from the government of the United Arab Emirates, a deal that will make the Trump family tens of millions of dollars per year from the investment. Laura Barron-Lopez, Ali Schmitz, and Courtney Norris, "Trump

Business Deals Revive Questions About His Family Profiting Off the Presidency," *PBS News Hour*, May 16, 2025, https://www.pbs.org/newshour/show/trump-business-deals-revive-questions-about-his-family-profiting-off-the-presidency.

OTHER REVENUE SOURCES

- *TIME* magazine found that Trump's financial disclosure lists him bringing in $3 million in income in fees from bibles, $1 million from sales of the "45" guitar, $2.8 million from Trump watches, and $2.5 million from Trump sneakers and fragrances. Brian Bennett, "3 Ways Trump's Wealth Has Soared Since He Returned to Office," *TIME*, December 29, 2025, https://time.com/7342470/trump-net-worth-wealth-crypto/.
- *Bloomberg* reported that digital assets added $1.4 billion to the first family's wealth over the past year, making up about one-fifth of their fortune for the first time. "Donald Trump Family Net-Worth Increasingly Comes from Crypto," *Bloomberg News*, January 20, 2026, https://www.bloomberg.com/news/features/2026-01-20/donald-trump-family-net-worth-increasingly-comes-from-crypto.

CONFLICT OF INTEREST CONCERNS

- PBS noted that, according to recent estimates, the Trump family and its partners have made some $320 million in trading fees since the president's meme coin launched, while Trump simultaneously promised to roll back oversight of the cryptocurrency industry. Laura Barron-Lopez, Ali Schmitz, and Courtney Norris, "Trump Business Deals Revive Questions About His Family Profiting Off the Presidency," *PBS News Hour*, May 16, 2025, https://www.pbs.org/newshour/show/trump-business-deals-revive-questions-about-his-family-profiting-off-the-presidency.
- The White House has consistently denied any conflicts of interest, with Press Secretary Karoline Leavitt stating that neither the president nor his family have engaged in conflicts of interest.

6. The evidence suggests Trump's policies have created opportunities for China and Russia to expand their influence precisely where America has withdrawn, fundamentally weakening US global standing.

CREATING VACUUMS FOR ADVERSARIES TO FILL

- *Newsweek* reported that former senior officials wrote in a court filing that the freeze on foreign aid "created vacuums of need all around the world, ceding influence and permitting China and Russia to seize those opportunities left behind." Former Defense Secretary Chuck Hagel stated, "When you abruptly cut off really important assistance, [other nations] lose confidence and trust in us. China and other nations will fill that vacuum." Daniel Bush, "Trump's USAID Cuts Help China and Russia, Former Officials Argue in Court," *Newsweek*, March 17, 2025, https://www.newsweek.com/usaid-trump-court-chuck-hagel-interview-2046127.
- NBC News reported that concerns are growing that temporarily halting assistance from USAID "opens up a window for China and Russia," with the decision leading to American influence waning in Africa, South America, and Asia. Chantal Da Silva, "What Cutting USAID Could Cost the U.S.—and How China, Russia May Benefit," NBC News, February 4, 2025, https://www.nbcnews.com/news/world/donald-trump-elon-musk-usaid-soft-power-china-russia-rcna189756.

MASSIVE CUTS TO FOREIGN AID

- The Council on Foreign Relations documented that for fiscal year 2025, enacted foreign aid dropped to $38.4 billion, with additional rescissions cutting this number by at least $9.4 billion. Funding for 2026 stands at $28.5 billion, with estimates as low as $8.1 billion, including rescissions and cancellations. Heidi E. Crebo-Rediker et al., "Visualizing 2026: Five Foreign Policy Trends to Watch," Council on Foreign Relations, December 17, 2025, https://www.cfr.org/articles/visualizing-2026-five-foreign-policy-trends-watch.

- The Center for American Progress reported that as of November 5, 2025, the elimination of USAID has resulted in six hundred thousand deaths, two-thirds of which were children. CAP National Security and International Policy Department, "Trump Global Weakness Watch: How Trump Is Undermining American Power," Center for American Progress, January 12, 2026, https://www.americanprogress.org/article/trump-global-weakness-watch-how-trump-is-undermining-american-power/.

UNDERMINING ALLIANCES AND SOFT POWER

- NPR quoted foreign policy expert Richard Haass explaining that, compared to Russia and China, "we get up every morning, and we have this enormous pool of allies who are willing to work with us." But Trump's foreign policy approach "treats allies just like everybody else, in some cases worse than everybody else." This could lead allies to diversify their portfolios rather than depending on the United States. Leila Fadel and Obed Manuel, "4 Thoughts on Trump's New World Order from Foreign Relations Expert Richard Haass," *NPR Morning Edition*, February 18, 2025, https://www.npr.org/2025/02/18/nx-s1-5299952/trump-foreign-policy-richard-haass-russia.
- *TIME* magazine reported that the Trump administration has essentially crossed out two of the three pillars of national power in diplomacy and development, pushing through sudden, debilitating cuts to foreign aid that triggered warnings of devastation and preventable deaths in the developing world. Brian Bennett and Nik Popli, "How Trump's Foreign Policy Gambits Are Reshaping the World," *Time*, January 15, 2026, https://time.com/collections/davos-2026/7345543/trump-foreign-policy-second-term/.

SHIFT TOWARD SPHERES OF INFLUENCE

- The Brookings Institution analyzed Trump's National Security Strategy, noting it adopts a notably more conciliatory tone toward competitors, framing the challenge as "managing European relations with Russia" and working to "rebalance America's economic relationship with China," with the document framing "the outsized influence of larger, richer, and stronger nations" as "a timeless truth of international relations," rejecting "global domination" in favor of "global and regional balances of power."

- This suggests the United States under Trump is less intent on strategic competition and more open to spheres of influence, effectively accepting Russian and Chinese regional dominance. Scott R. Anderson, "Breaking Down Trump's 2025 National Security Strategy: Brookings Experts Weigh In," Brookings Institution, December 8, 2025, https://www.brookings.edu/articles/breaking-down-trumps-2025-national-security-strategy/.

LOSS OF GLOBAL INFLUENCE

- The Center for American Progress stated that as Trump retreats from global leadership, adversaries such as China and Russia have stepped in—not because they are stronger, but because the United States is leaving a vacuum. According to a 2025 Pew Research Center study, global confidence in US leadership has plummeted. CAP National Security and International Policy Department, "Trump Global Weakness Watch: How Trump Is Undermining American Power," Center for American Progress, January 12, 2026, https://www.americanprogress.org/article/trump-global-weakness-watch-how-trump-is-undermining-american-power/.

7. Roland Rajah and Ahmed Albaryrak, "China Versus America on Global Trade: China's Unbalanced Global Trading Relationships Have Only Deepened," Lowy Institute, January 2025, https://interactives.lowyinstitute.org/features/china-versus-america-on-global-trade/#map.
8. Donald J. Trump and Tony Schwartz, *Trump: The Art of the Deal* (Ballantine Books, 2015), 58.
9. Trump has convinced his supporters that his prosecutions are political persecution rather than legitimate legal accountability.

The strategy works by creating an alternate reality where any accountability for Trump is reframed as an attack on his supporters, making his legal troubles their shared grievance against a corrupt elite.

POPULIST "US VERSUS THEM" FRAMING

- Wikipedia documented that Trump portrayed himself as a victim of the "Deep State" actively attempting to undermine him and the country. His criminal trials made him, in his words, a "political prisoner," similar to Alexei Navalny. He framed a common theme in his rallies as the struggle between "us" (the majority, or his supporters) and "them" (the elites, or his political enemies). Wikipedia, "Donald Trump 2024 Presidential Campaign," last modified March 16, 2026, 21:17 (UTC), https://en.wikipedia.org/wiki/Donald_Trump_2024_presidential_campaign.
- CNN analysis determined that Trump voters respond to his populism and his evisceration of elites, and many sincerely believe he's a response to the Democratic Party's march to the left. Trump's castigation of what the "establishment" sees as truth is not a bug—it's the key feature of his appeal. Stephen Collinson, "Trump Seeds Disinformation as He Sets Course for a Possible Oval Office Return," CNN, October 8, 2024, https://www.cnn.com/2024/10/08/politics/trump-disinformation-2024-analysis/index.html.

POSITIONING HIMSELF AS ONE OF THE PEOPLE

- *Springer Nature* research found that Trump supporters said things like "I don't really look at him as a politician. . . . I look at him as just one of us. He doesn't act like he's above you, as a person." The study noted that Trump rails against the political establishment, the media, and the progressive intelligentsia; professes to be the voice of all true Americans; stokes nationalistic and nativist sentiments; and tries, by his folksiness of demeanor and informality of expression, to convince the average Joe that he is just like him. Jens

Kjeldgaard-Christiansen, "The Voice of the People: Populism and Donald Trump's Use of Informal Voice," *Springer Social Science and Modern Society* 61 (2024): 289–302, https://doi.org/10.1007/s12115-024-00969-7.

RESONATING WITH COMMUNITIES FAMILIAR WITH PERSECUTION

- ABC News reported that Trump sharpened his rhetoric of alleged persecution and resistance to Communism, invoking the experiences of Cuban immigrants who fled Castro. Rally attendees said Trump's messaging persuaded them, with one immigrant stating through tears that she believed Trump's criminal charges were brought for political reasons. Lalee Ibssa and Soo Rin Kim, "Trump Paints Himself as a Victim in Pitch to Florida Hispanics Wary of Political Persecution," ABC News, November 9, 2023, https://abcnews.com/Politics/trump-paints-victim-pitch-florida-hispanics-wary-political/story?id=104722015.

RELIGIOUS PERSECUTION NARRATIVE

- NPR examined how Trump says he's being persecuted, and that idea resonates with his Christian base, with the idea of persecution holding a particular meaning for Christians. Ari Shapiro, host, *Consider This*, podcast, "Why Trump's Persecution Narrative Resonates with Christian Supporters," NPR, February 2, 2024, https://www.npr.org/2024/02/02/1198910302/consider-this-from-npr-draft-02-02-2024.
- The messaging tapped into Christian nationalism, alleging that Christianity was being besieged and Christians were facing persecution by Democrats, and that he would guard it and reclaim its rightful role in US society. Wikipedia, "Donald Trump 2024 Presidential Campaign," last modified March 16, 2026, 21:17 (UTC), https://en.wikipedia.org/wiki/Donald_Trump_2024_presidential_campaign.

"DEEP STATE" AND ELITE CONSPIRACY FRAMING

- *The Cornell Daily Sun* explained that the Deep State conspiracy theory suggests there is a network of individuals in the federal government that are working together with elite leaders furthering their own agenda regardless of the people's needs. This theory became very popular during Trump's first term when he claimed that it was working against him. Sophia Romanov Imber, "Plato's Cave and Trump's Next Term," *Cornell Daily Sun*, November 11, 2024, https://www.cornellsun.com/article/2024/11/platos-cave-and-trumps-next-term.

- NPR reported that replacement theory fits into an array of fears that GOP elected officials and right-wing media outlets like Fox News have stoked around the theme that political elites, a shadowy cabal of power brokers, are trying to rob Americans of something they hold dear. Jude Joffe-Block and Odette Yousef, "How Trump Is Relying on a Racist Conspiracy Theory to Question Election Results," NPR, September 13, 2024, https://www.npr.org/2024/09/13/g-s1-22583/trump-great-replacement-conspiracy-theory.

MARTYRDOM AND VICTIMHOOD MESSAGING

- Wikipedia noted that Trump framed the election as "the final battle" and his presidential campaign as a "righteous crusade" against "atheists, globalists and the Marxists." He referred to January 6 Capitol attack participants as patriotic "warriors" and "hostages," symbols of political injustice. Wikipedia, "Donald Trump 2024 Presidential Campaign," last modified March 16, 2026, 21:17 (UTC), https://en.wikipedia.org/wiki/Donald_Trump_2024_presidential_campaign.

CONSTANT REPETITION DESPITE CONTRADICTORY EVIDENCE

- CNN observed that Trump is certain to claim that he is being politically victimized. This not only has the political effect of solidifying Trump's appeal to supporters as he claims he's a victim of witch hunts, but also bolsters his long-term attempts to create a public narrative that any future convictions against him will be unjust. Stephen Collinson, "Trump State Prosecutions Reach a Critical Point on the Same Day in

Two Cities," CNN, February 15, 2025, https://www.cnn.com/2024/02/15/politics/trump-state-prosecutions-new-york-georgia/index.html.

THE IRONY

- NPR documented that Trump himself has repeatedly claimed he was the victim of political persecution by Democrats while simultaneously issuing threats to prosecute political rivals and reposting messages demanding arrests of poll workers, judges, and prosecutors. Tom Dreisbach, "Trump Has Made More Than 100 Threats to Prosecute or Punish Perceived Enemies," NPR, October 22, 2024, https://www.npr.org/2024/10/21/nx-s1-5134924/trump-election-2024-kamala-harris-elizabeth-cheney-threat-civil-liberties.

10. Extensive documentation shows a decades-long pattern of Trump using the threat of expensive litigation, character attacks, and financial ruin to avoid paying bills, silence critics, and extract settlements. Jeff Spross, "A Brief History of Trump's Small-Time Swindles: A Certain Commander in Chief Has a Long History of Being Accused of Screwing Over the Little Guy," *The Week*, July 11, 2018, https://theweek.com/articles/783976/brief-history-trumps-smalltime-swindles.

PATTERN OF NOT PAYING CONTRACTORS

- A *USA Today* investigation found that hundreds of workers and contractors have accused Donald Trump of not paying his bills over the years; hundreds of liens and judgments, and at least sixty lawsuits, against him and his businesses allege that he has not fully paid workers for their labor. The report found a tendency for Trump's businesses to engage in lengthy legal battles over relatively small dollar figures, often reaching settlements that require confidentiality from the plaintiffs. Harper Neidig, "Report: Trump Has Refused to Pay Hundreds of Workers," *The Hill*, June 9, 2016, https://thehill.com/blogs/ballot-box/presidential-races/282933-report-trump-has-refused-to-pay-hundreds-of-workers/.

- Fox News reported that a former Trump Plaza executive stated, "Part of how he did business as a philosophy was to negotiate the best price he could. And then when it came time to pay the bills, Trump would say 'I'm going to pay you but I'm going to pay you 75% of what we agreed to.'" Fox News, "Dozens of Lawsuits Accuse Trump of Not Paying His Bills, Reports Claim," June 10, 2016, https://www.foxnews.com/politics/dozens-of-lawsuits-accuse-trump-of-not-paying-his-bills-reports-claim.

USING LEGAL THREATS TO INTIMIDATE

- Paul Friel told CNN his dad's small business went under at the hands of the billionaire when Trump refused to pay $84,000 for completed cabinet work, with Friel suspecting that Trump also used his clout in the industry to block the company from getting other Atlantic City contracts. Laura Dolan and Jessica Schneider, "The Small Business Owners Trump Never Paid in Full," CNN, September 14, 2016, https://www.cnn.com/2016/09/13/politics/trump-small-business-owners.
- The United Steelworkers described Trump's approach: Pillage is Trump's business model. United Steel Worker's International President, "Billionaire Trump Fleeces Workers, Small Businesses," *President's Perspective* (blog), USW.org, June 21, 2016, https://usw.org/billionaire-trump-fleeces-workers-small-businesses/.
- Trump has been embroiled in hundreds of lawsuits for refusal to pay contractors and workers at his projects across the country. Steve Reilly, "*USA TODAY* Exclusive: Hundreds Allege Donald Trump Doesn't Pay His Bills," *USA Today*, June 9, 2016, https://www.usatoday.com/story/news/politics/elections/2016/06/09/donald-trump-unpaid-bills-republican-president-laswuits/85297274/.

SLAPP LAWSUITS AS INTIMIDATION

- The Public Participation Project reported that Trump bragged about one lawsuit: "I spent a couple of bucks on legal fees, and they spent a whole lot more. I did it to make his life miserable, which I'm happy about." Public Participation Project, "Former President Trump and the First Amendment: What You Need to Know," Anti-SLAPP.org, https://anti-slapp.org/trump-and-the-first-amendment.

- *The Conversation* explained that even if Trump loses lawsuits, he has inflicted expensive litigation costs on news organizations, and if even media giants such as ABC and CBS are settling rather than fighting, what local news editor is going to assign a story that might trigger a presidential lawsuit? Kathy Kiely and Lyrissa Barnett Lidsky, "Trump Lawsuits Seek to Muzzle Media, Posing Serious Threat to Free Press," *The Conversation*, January 12, 2026, https://theconversation.com/trump-lawsuits-seek-to-muzzle-media-posing-serious-threat-to-free-press-272850.
- FIRE noted that Trump has a very poor track record in civil lawsuits, particularly those claiming defamation. In fact, he nearly always loses—sometimes very badly. Trump has even been ordered to pay media defendants substantial damages for filing harassing and frivolous defamation lawsuits. Ronald Collins, "Executive Watch: Trump's Weaponization of Civil Lawsuits—First Amendment News 462," Foundation for Individual Rights and Expression (FIRE), March 18, 2025, https://www.thefire.org/news/blogs/ronald-kl-collins-first-amendment-news/executive-watch-trumps-weaponization-civil.

CHARACTER ASSASSINATION TACTICS

- Crush The LSAT documented a case where financial analyst Marvin B. Roffman was fired from his position due to harsh criticism and multiple lawsuit threats from Trump after Roffman predicted the Trump Taj Mahal would fail. After being constantly badmouthed by Trump in the press, Roffman filed a $2 million defamation suit against Trump to defend his professional reputation. Bryce Welker, "Donald Trump Settlement and Lawsuits, History of Legal Affairs," Crush the LSAT, February 14, 2026, https://crushthelsatexam.com/deep-dive-donald-trumps-long-history-of-lawsuits/.

USING GOVERNMENT POWER TO INTIMIDATE

- Under Trump's second administration, legal experts stated that targeting of lawyers and law firms for the clients they represent could intimidate lawyers from representing certain clients in the future. A judge stated the orders "casts a chilling harm of blizzard proportion across the entire legal profession." Wikipedia, "Targeting of Law Firms and Lawyers Under the Second Trump Administration," last modified March 15, 2026, 15:20 (UTC), https://en.wikipedia.org/wiki/Targeting_of_law_firms_and_lawyers_under_the_second_Trump_administration.
- MS NOW reported that Trump's lawsuit template against media organizations works as an extortion scheme: Trump finds some offense, claims he has been terribly wounded, and demands a huge payout. The targets, fearing what could happen to their businesses, pony up millions in settlements. He got payouts from CBS ($16 million), ABC ($15 million), Meta ($25 million), YouTube ($24.5 million), and Twitter/X ($10 million). Paul Waldman, "Trump's $10 Billion IRS Lawsuit Is Unlike Anything He's Filed Before," MS NOW, February 1, 2026, https://www.ms.now/opinion/trump-10-billion-irs-lawsuit-taxes-corrupt. See also Jeff Spross, "A Brief History of Trump's Small-Time Swindles: A Certain Commander in Chief Has a Long History of Being Accused of Screwing Over the Little Guy," *The Week*, July 11, 2018, https://theweek.com/articles/783976/brief-history-trumps-smalltime-swindles.

11. A University of Michigan Law School journal documented that the Muslim ban had an immediate impact on tens of thousands of Muslims, directly affecting US visa and green card holders currently outside of the country, while exacerbating fear and hysteria among immigrant and citizen Muslim populations

within the country. Abed Ayoub and Khaled Beydoun, "Executive Disorder: The Muslim Ban, Emergency Advocacy, and the Fires Next Time," *Michigan Journal of Race & Law* 22, no. 2 (2017), https://repository.law.umich.edu/mjrl/vol22/iss2/2/.

12. NBC News reported that in January of 2019 the president asked for $5.7 billion to build "a steel barrier for the Southwest border," but Congress approved only $1.375 billion. In February 2019, Trump declared a national emergency and ordered that money for Pentagon construction projects would be used instead for the wall. Pete Williams, "Judge Rules Trump Violated the Law on Wall Funding with National Emergency," NBC News, October 11, 2019, https://www.nbcnews.com/politics/immigration/judge-rules-trump-violated-law-wall-funding-national-emergency-n1065216.

13. Trump's Deep State narrative has been a central theme of his political messaging, casting career government officials, law enforcement, and intelligence agencies as part of a coordinated conspiracy against him and his supporters.

DIRECT REFERENCES TO "DEEP STATE" AND "ENEMY WITHIN"

- *The Cornell Daily Sun* documented that the Deep State conspiracy theory suggests there is a network of individuals in the federal government working together with elite leaders furthering their own agenda regardless of the people's needs. The Deep State became very popular during Trump's first term when he claimed that it was working against him and his administration. And in 2024, Trump has discussed "the enemy within" that opposes him and that he believes it needs to be "handled" by military force if necessary. Sophia Romanov Imber, "Plato's Cave and Trump's Next Term," *The Cornell Daily Sun*, November 11, 2024, https://www.cornellsun.com/article/2024/11/platos-cave-and-trumps-next-term.

PORTRAYING HIMSELF AS VICTIM

- Wikipedia's coverage of Trump's 2024 campaign noted that Trump portrayed himself as a victim of the Deep State actively attempting to undermine him and the country. Wikipedia, "Donald Trump 2024 Presidential Campaign," last modified March 16, 2026, 21:17 (UTC), https://en.wikipedia.org/wiki/Donald_Trump_2024_presidential_campaign.

ACCUSATIONS AGAINST LAW ENFORCEMENT

- NPR reported that Trump has repeatedly accused the Biden administration of "weaponizing" the Justice Department and subjecting him to "political persecution" and a "witch hunt," framing investigations of Trump as politically motivated rather than legitimate law enforcement. Tom Dreisbach, "Trump Has Made More Than 100 Threats to Prosecute or Punish Perceived Enemies," NPR, October 22, 2024, https://www.npr.org/2024/10/21/nx-s1-5134924/trump-election-2024-kamala-harris-elizabeth-cheney-threat-civil-liberties.
- NPR also documented that throughout his presidential campaign, Trump claimed he was the victim of political persecution by Democrats positioning government agencies as tools of political opponents rather than independent institutions. Tom Dreisbach, "Trump Has Used Government Powers to Target More Than 100 Perceived Enemies," NPR, April 29, 2025, https://www.npr.org/2025/04/29/nx-s1-5327518/donald-trump-100-days-retribution-threats.

CONSPIRACY AS POLITICAL MESSAGING

- Academic research on Trump's populism found that Trump's communicative strategy created an imaginary community based on radical exclusion and antagonistic frontiers, fostering a belief in the possibility that this imagined community can return to sovereignty by defeating establishment elites. Alexandra Homolar and Ronny Scholz, "The Power of Trump-Speak: Populist Crisis Narratives and Ontological Security," *Cambridge Review of International Affairs* 32, no. 3 (2019): 344–364, https://doi.org/10.1080/09557571.2019.1575796.

14. Jeremy Diamond, "Trump Sides with Putin over US intelligence," CNN, July 16, 2018, https://www.cnn.com/2018/07/16/politics/donald-trump-putin-helsinki-summit.

15. Jessica Piper and Renee Klahr, "'I' and 'Me': How Trump's Second Inaugural Speech Is Different from 'American Carnage,'" *Politico*, January 20, 2025, https://www.politico.com/news/2025/01/20/5-ways-trumps-second-inaugural-address-was-different-from-his-first-00199436.
16. Paul Dans and Steven Groves, eds., *Mandate for Leadership: The Conservative Promise* (Washington, DC: The Heritage Foundation, 2023), https://static.heritage.org/project2025/2025_MandateForLeadership_FULL.pdf.
17. Donald Trump (@realDonaldTrump), "I have a meeting today with Russ Vought, of PROJECT 2025 Fame, to determine which of the many Democrat Agencies, most of which are a political SCAM, he recommends to be cut, and whether or not those cuts will be temporary or permanent. I can't believe the Radical Left Democrats gave me this unprecedented opportunity. They are not stupid people, so maybe this is their way of wanting to, quietly and quickly, MAKE AMERICA GREAT AGAIN!," Truth Social, October 2, 2025, https://truthsocial.com/@realDonaldTrump/posts/115304455138824245.
18. Trump's administration implemented budget cuts exceeding $1 billion, reduced staff by over 24 percent (approximately four thousand permanent employees), and caused closures to trails, visitor centers, and campgrounds while jeopardizing operations at hundreds of park sites nationwide.

BUDGET CUTS OVER $1 BILLION

- The Trump administration's proposed 2026 budget includes an unprecedented scale of cuts for the agencies that manage America's outdoor spaces, campgrounds, trails, wildlife, and more. In total, the proposed budget includes a nearly $4 billion cut to national parks, national forests, wildlife refuges, wilderness and recreation areas, and more. That is a 35 percent decrease from 2024 funding. Sam Zeno and Jenny Rowland-Shea, "The Trump Administration Is Recklessly Axing Funding and Staff for America's National Parks, Forests, and Public Lands," Center for American Progress, July 1,

2025, https://www.americanprogress.org/article/the-trump-administration-is-recklessly-axing-funding-and-staff-for-americas-national-parks-forests-and-public-lands/.

- "President Trump's reduced budget proposal calls for a cut of more than $1 billion to the National Park Service, which includes a $900 million cut to the operations of our national parks—the largest proposed cut in the Park Service's 109-year history." National Parks Conservation Association, "President Trump's Proposed Budget Could Decimate At Least 350 National Park Sites," press release, May 5, 2025, https://www.npca.org/articles/8495-president-trump-s-proposed-budget-could-decimate-at-least-350-national-park.
- "Trump's proposed big, beautiful budget bill for the current fiscal year would rescind more than $250 million in funding that pays for rangers, emergency responders and scientists. And next year, he wants to cut $1.2 billion more." Kirk Siegler, "Trump's Efforts to Cut National Parks Budget Faces Bipartisan Pushback," NPR, June 10, 2025, https://www.npr.org/2025/06/10/nx-s1-5424547-e1/trumps-efforts-to-cut-national-parks-budget-faces-bipartisan-pushback.

CLOSURES AND REDUCED SERVICES

- "Without NPS staff, visitor centers will be closed during the height of the tourism season, restrooms will be left dirty, and tours will be left unfinished." US Senator Ed Markey, "Senator Markey Decries Trump Administration Cuts to National Park Service and Attacks on Massachusetts Economy, Heritage," February 25, 2025, https://www.markey.senate.gov/news/press-releases/senator-markey-decries-trump-administration-cuts-to-national-park-service-and-attacks-on-massachusetts-economy-heritage.

IMPACT ON HUNDREDS OF PARK SITES

- "The National Parks Conservation Association (NPCA) has calculated the Trump administration's proposed cuts to the National Park Service budget could result in more than a 75% reduction to the National Park System. With 433 national park units across the country, that would essentially wipe out budgets and staffing for at least 350 national park units." National Parks Conservation Association, "President Trump's Proposed Budget Could Decimate At Least 350 National Park Sites," press release, May 5, 2025, https://www.npca.org/articles/8495-president-trump-s-proposed-budget-could-decimate-at-least-350-national-park.

19. Rick Claypool, "Trump's Billionaire Cabinet Represents the Top 0.0001%," *Public Citizen*, January 14, 2025, https://www.citizen.org/article/trumps-billionaire-cabinet-represents-the-top-0001-percent/.

20. Immigration detention statistics via TracReports show that of the 70,766 people detained by ICE as of February 7, 2026, approximately 74 percent of those detained had no criminal convictions, and many of those with "criminal convictions" were convicted of minor offenses including traffic violations. Transactional Records Access Clearinghouse, "Immigration Detention Quick Facts," last modified February 7, 2026, https://tracreports.org/immigration/quickfacts/#:~:text=65%2C135,see%20more%20data.

21. Courtney Kube, Gordon Lubold, and Carol E. Lee, "Trump White House Has Asked U.S. Military to Develop Options for the Panama Canal, Officials Say," NBC News, March 13, 2025, https://www.nbcnews.com/politics/national-security/trump-white-house-asked-us-military-develop-options-panama-canal-offic-rcna195994.

22. Jeff Mason, Andrew Hay, and Diego Ore, "Trump Frees Honduran Leader Convicted on Cocaine Charges, Sparks Outcry from Democrats," Reuters, December 2, 2025, https://www.reuters.com/world/americas/former-honduran-president-released-us-prison-after-trump-pardon-2025-12-02/.

23. The six Democratic lawmakers who appeared in the video were all military veterans or former intelligence officers: Senators Mark Kelly (Arizona) and Elissa Slotkin (Michigan), and Representatives Jason Crow (Colorado), Chris Deluzio (Pennsylvania), Chrissy

Houlahan (Pennsylvania), and Maggie Goodlander (New Hampshire). In the video, they reminded military service members that "You can refuse illegal orders. You must refuse illegal orders."

Following Trump's threats, the administration took several actions. Defense Secretary Pete Hegseth moved to demote Kelly's military retirement rank and reduce his pension, though a federal judge ruled that this "trampled" on Kelly's First Amendment rights and blocked the Pentagon's actions. Gary Grumbach and Ryan J. Reilly, "Judge Says Pentagon 'Trampled' on Sen. Mark Kelly's Rights, Blocks Effort to Demote Him over 'Illegal Orders' Video," NBC News, February 12, 2026, https://www.nbcnews.com/politics/justice-department/judge-blocks-mark-kelly-demotion-illegal-orders-rcna258777.

The Trump administration's US attorney for DC, Jeanine Pirro, attempted to secure a grand jury indictment against the lawmakers but failed because they couldn't get a grand jury to support it. S. E. Cupp, "Leave It to Trump, Hegseth to Raise Presidential Profile of Democratic Arizona Sen. Mark Kelly," *Chicago Sun-Times*, February 13, 2026, https://chicago.suntimes.com/columnists/2026/02/13/trump-hegseth-military-illegal-orders-mark-kelly-democrats-2028-cupp.

Kelly filed a lawsuit and has successfully blocked the administration's attempts to punish him for the video so far.

24. Fareed Zakaria, "Populists Are Replacing Meritocracy with Something Far Worse," *Washington Post*, December 5, 2025, https://www.washingtonpost.com/opinions/2025/12/05/trump-plutocrat-meritocracy-experts/.

25. Deutsche Bank loaned Trump over $2 billion despite numerous red flags, including inflated financial statements, forged documents, previous defaults, and his status as a client rejected by other major banks. "Deutsche Bank Loaned Trump $2bn Despite Multiple Red Flags, New Report Claims," *World Finance*, February 12, 2026, https://www.worldfinance.com/strategy/deutsche-bank-loaned-trump-2bn-despite-multiple-red-flags-new-report-claims.

26. Paul Kiel and Russ Buettner, "IRS Audit of Trump Could Cost Former President More Than $100 Million," *ProPublica* and *New York Times*, May 11, 2024, https://www.propublica.org/article/trump-irs-audit-chicago-hotel-taxes.

27. References to Trump's operational style often liken it to that of a mob boss.
    - The abstract for a scholarly analysis published in an MDPI journal states: "This article comprehensively examines Donald Trump's political leadership, arguing that his tenure as the 45th President of the United States exhibited characteristics commonly associated with authoritarian mob bosses and notes the hierarchical makeup of Trump's leadership style and chain of command, with Jared Kushner and Donald Trump Jr.'s major roles in political strategy and business making them underbosses." Najja K. Baptist and Kenneth A. Clark, "Unmasking the Authoritarian Mob Boss: A Critical Analysis of Donald Trump's Political Leadership," *Social Sciences* 13, no. 8 (2024): 397, https://www.mdpi.com/2076-0760/13/8/397.
    - "Trump operates like a mob boss, surrounding himself with family members and groveling loyalists, prizing fealty above all else, and practicing a transactional politics of favors and deals that shows little regard for legal norms." Jeet Heer, "Donald Trump's Government of Gangsters," *The Nation*, December 2, 2024, https://www.thenation.com/article/society/trump-gravano-government-gangsters/.
    - "The metaphor of the mafia boss fits this logic: Loyalty is rewarded, resistance is met with intimidation, and promises are often broken." Rafael Pampillon, "Trump as a Mafia Boss," *IE Insights*, September 22, 2025, https://www.ie.edu/insights/articles/trump-as-a-mafia-boss/.

28. US Senator Marco Rubio, "Rubio Campaign Press Release—The Four Times Donald Trump Has Declared Bankruptcy," American Presidency Project, February 26, 2016, https://www.presidency.ucsb.edu/documents/rubio-campaign-press-release-the-four-times-donald-trump-has-declared-bankruptcy.

29. Robert Maguire and Rebecca Jacobs, "Trump Likely Benefited from $13.6 Million in Payments from Foreign Governments During His Presidency," Citizens for Ethics Crew Report, September 17, 2024, https://www.citizensforethics.org/reports-investigations/crew-reports/trump-likely-benefited-from-13-6-million-in-payments-from-foreign-governments-during-his-presidency/.

30. Beth Reinhard et al., "How Billionaires Took Over American Politics," *Washington Post*, November 21, 2025, https://www.washingtonpost.com/politics/interactive/2025/billionaires-politics-money-influence/.

31. Talva Minsberg, "A Timeline of Trump's On-Again, Off-Again Tariffs: The President's Penchant for Imposing and Then Suspending Tariffs Has Shaken Markets and Confounded Trading Partners," *New York Times*, March 13, 2025, https://www.nytimes.com/2025/03/13/business/economy/trump-tariff-timeline.html.

32. "President Donald J. Trump Achieved the Biggest Tax Cuts and Reforms in American History," Trump White House Archives, February 5, 2025, https://trumpwhitehouse.archives.gov/briefings-statements/president-donald-j-trump-achieved-biggest-tax-cuts-reforms-american-history/.

33. Patrick Villanova and Marie White, eds., "Trump Tax Brackets: Will Your Tax Rate Change Under the New Plan?," *SmartAsset*, last modified March 12, 2026, https://smartasset.com/taxes/trump-tax-brackets.

34. Dharna Noor, "Big Oil Spent $445m in Last Election Cycle to Influence Trump and Congress, Report Says," *The Guardian*, January 23, 2025, https://www.theguardian.com/us-news/2025/jan/23/big-oil-445m-trump-congress.

35. Oskar Dye-Furstenberg, "The Hollow Energy Agenda of Trump's First Four Months," Roosevelt Institute, May 29, 2025, https://rooseveltinstitute.org/blog/the-hollow-energy-agenda-of-trump/.

36. "U.S. Crude Output Jumps to Record 11.35 Million bpd in August: EIA," Reuters, October 31, 2018, https://www.reuters.com/article/us-usa-oil-production/us-crude-output-jumps-to-record-1135-million-bpd-in-august-eia-idUSKCN1N52FH/; Robert Rapier, "Which President Oversaw the Largest Changes in U.S. Oil Production?" *Forbes*, March 16, 2023, https://www.forbes.com/sites/rrapier/2023/03/16/which-president-oversaw-the-largest-changes-in-us-oil-production/.
37. Naveena Sadasivam Grist, "2025: The Year the US Gave Up on Climate, and the World Gave Up on Us," *DC Report*, December 13, 2025, https://www.dcreport.org/2025/12/13/2025-the-year-the-us-gave-up-on-climate-and-the-world-gave-up-on-us/.
38. Anushree Jonko, ed., "'I Am A Dictator, Sometimes You Need One': Trump After Davos Speech," NDTV World, January 22, 2026, https://www.ndtv.com/world-news/i-am-a-dictator-sometimes-you-need-one-donald-trump-says-after-davos-speech-10832557.
39. Thom Hartmann, *The Last American President: A Broken Man, a Corrupt Party, and a World on the Brink* (Berrett-Koehler Publishers, 2025).
40. USA Facts Team, "Who Owns American Wealth? As of 2023, the Top 1% of American Households Owned 30 Cents of Every Dollar," *USA Facts*, August 7, 2024, https://usafacts.org/articles/who-owns-american-wealth/.
41. Chase Peterson-Withorn, ed., with Matt Durot, "Forbes 400: The Definitive Ranking of America's Richest People 2025," *Forbes*, https://www.forbes.com/forbes-400/.
42. Michael Hirchorn, "The Billionaires Have Gone Full Louis XV," *New York Times*, December 14, 2025, https://www.nytimes.com/2025/12/14/opinion/billionaires-politics-money.html?smid=em-share.
43. "Public Statement: Human Rights Organizations in Ecuador Denounce Police Takeover of Indigenous Headquarters," Mining Watch Canada, July 23, 2024, https://miningwatch.ca/news/2024/7/23/public-statement-human-rights-organizations-ecuador-denounce-police-takeover.

44. "Solaris Highlights Strength and Global Scale of US$3.7bn Mining Project in Ecuador," BNamericas, November 11, 2025, https://www.bnamericas.com/en/features/solaris-resources-estimates-1300mt-copper-reserves-in-us37bn-ecuadorian-project.
45. Eli Pearl, "Operation Condor and the Horrors of US Foreign Policy," Institute for Youth and Policy, July 12, 2021, https://yipinstitute.org/article/operation-condor-and-the-horrors-of-u-s-foreign-policy.
46. Isabela Dias, "Gringos, Go Home: Latin America Reacts to Trump's Expanding Military Campaign," *Mother Jones*, October 25, 2025, https://www.motherjones.com/politics/2025/10/gringos-go-home-latin-america-reacts-to-trumps-expanding-military-campaign/.
47. Ibid.
48. "Trump Says U.S. Will Run Venezuela After U.S. Captures Maduro," Reuters, January 3, 2026, https://www.reuters.com/world/americas/loud-noises-heard-venezuela-capital-southern-area-without-electricity-2026-01-03/.
49. Sophia Compton, "Trump Announces $100B Oil Investment Plan for Venezuela Following Maduro's Capture," Fox Business, January 9, 2026, https://www.foxbusiness.com/politics/trump-announces-100b-oil-investment-plan-venezuela-following-maduros-capture.
50. Julian E. Zelizer, "What Kent State Taught the Country About State Violence," *Foreign Policy*, January 26, 2026, https://foreignpolicy.com/2026/01/26/kent-state-violence-minneapolis/.
51. Chabeli Carrazana, "Here's What's Really Happening with Child Care Fraud in Minnesota," *19th News*, January 9, 2026, https://19thnews.org/2026/01/child-care-fraud-minnesota-fact-check/.

Index

E

About the Author

After business school and serving as a Peace Corps volunteer deep in the Amazon rainforest, John Perkins lived four lives: as chief economist of a major consulting firm, where his actual job was that of an economic hit man; as CEO of a successful alternative energy company, where he was rewarded for not disclosing his economic hit man past; as a teacher and writer who used his expertise on Indigenous cultures to promote environmental and cultural sustainability while continuing to honor his vows of silence about his economic hit man life; and now as a writer and activist, who, in telling the real-life story about his extraordinary experiences, exposed the world of international intrigue and corruption that used the EHM strategy to turn the American republic into a global empire.

John's job involved convincing lower-income countries to accept enormous loans for infrastructure projects that profited US businesses. Once those countries were saddled with debt, US corporations exploited their oil and other resources.

As detailed in his groundbreaking *Confessions of an Economic Hit Man* trilogy, John participated—directly or behind the scenes—in some of the most dramatic events in modern history, including the Saudi Arabian Money-Laundering Affair, the rise and fall of the shah of Iran, the suspicious deaths of Ecuador's president Jaime Roldós and Panama's Omar Torrijos, the lead-up to the US invasion of Panama, and actions that resulted in the 2003 Iraq war.

In *The Art of the Steal*, he draws on his economic hit man experiences to describe how US presidents of both parties have applied the four pillars of the EHM strategy (fear, debt, anxiety over insufficiency, and divide and conquer) to control other nations and enrich a growing oligarchy. As John demonstrates through multiple examples, Donald Trump represents a historic shift. He is the first US president to have turned the EHM strategy into a personal brand and governing style. He brought the economic hit man playbook home and reversed the march toward the American Ideal of liberty, equality, justice, democracy, opportunity, and an individualism that supports family and community. He has exposed a system that previously was hidden.

The Art of the Steal explains how this happened, why it matters, and what each of us can do to turn things around. Both warning and blueprint, it offers a pathway to renewing the American Ideal—and using it to model a Global Ideal.

After leaving the economic hit man ranks, John founded Independent Power Systems, Inc. (IPS), an alternative energy company. Under his leadership, IPS was extremely successful in a high-risk business. Many "coincidences" and favors from people in powerful positions helped make IPS an industry leader. When he began to write about economic hit men and the "jackals" who foment coups and assassinations, his life and that of his infant daughter were threatened. He took what amounted to a legal bribe: accepting a job as a highly paid consultant in exchange for not writing the book.

During the 1990s, John assuaged his guilt by founding or cofounding the nonprofit organizations Dream Change and the

Pachamama Alliance. He applied his consultant's fees to championing Indigenous rights and environmental movements, working especially closely with Amazonian nations.

The events of September 11, 2001, convinced John to ignore the threats and bribes and write *Confessions of an Economic Hit Man.* It became an international bestseller in thirty-eight languages, spent seventy-three weeks on *The New York Times* bestseller list, has sold millions of copies, and launched John on a global speaking tour to corporate summits, consumer and environmental conferences, music festivals, and more than fifty universities.

John has been featured on ABC, NBC, CNN, CNBC, NPR, A&E, and the History Channel; in *Time, The New York Times, The Washington Post, Cosmopolitan, Elle, Der Spiegel,* and many other publications; as well as in numerous documentaries. He was awarded the Lennon Ono Grant for Peace and the Rainforest Action Network Challenging Business as Usual Award.

Since the first *Confessions of an Economic Hit Man,* he has written *The Secret History of the American Empire* (Penguin), *Hoodwinked* (Random House), *The New Confessions of an Economic Hit Man* (Berrett-Koehler), *Touching the Jaguar* (Berrett-Koehler), and *Confessions of an Economic Hit Man,* 3rd Edition (Berrett-Koehler) about China's EHM strategy. He is also the author of books on Indigenous cultures and transformation, including *Shapeshifting, The World Is As You Dream It, Psychonavigation, Spirit of the Shuar,* and *The Stress-Free Habit* (all from Inner Traditions, Bear and Company), and a novel, *Message from Pleiades* (Eagle Harbour Publishing under the pen name JP Moody, digital only).

To learn more about John, find out where he is lecturing, order his books, subscribe to his newsletter, or contact him, please visit JohnPerkins.org.

To discover more about Dream Change and the Pachamama Alliance, please go to dreamchange.org and pachamama.org.

Be sure to see the documentary film about John Perkins

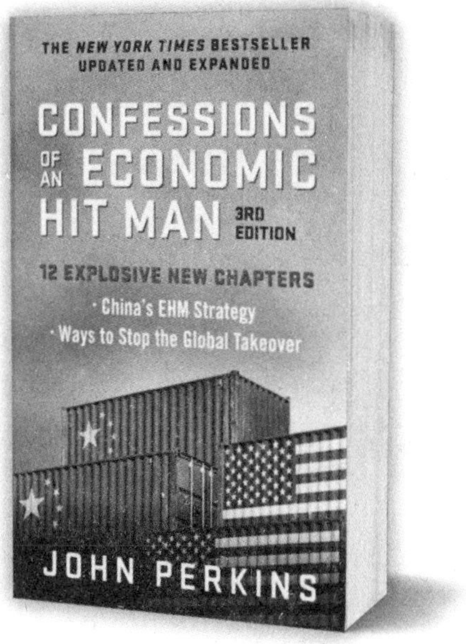

Based on the groundbreaking book, *Confessions of an Economic Hitman*, a soon-to-be released, gripping, globe-spanning documentary follows bestselling author John Perkins as he confronts the shadowy world he once helped build—a system where corporate interests, political power, and economic manipulation reshaped nations under the guise of development. Through intimate interviews, stylized animations, and an immersive journey back to the Amazon rainforest—Perkins retraces the path from ambitious young economist to whistleblower, revealing how debt, deception, and hidden "jackals" enforced a quiet empire across the world.

But this is more than a story of corruption—it is a story of transformation. As Perkins revisits the landscapes and people who changed him forever, the film evolves into a deeply personal quest for redemption, healing, and climate awareness. Guided by the spiritual philosophy of "Touching the Jaguar," he confronts his past while passing the torch to the next generation—culminating in a powerful return to the Amazon that redefines legacy, responsibility, and humanity's relationship with Mother Earth.

Also by John Perkins

Confessions of an Economic Hit Man, 3rd Edition

How do we confront the ever-evolving economic hit man strategy—and China's expanding global influence? In this riveting third edition of the *New York Times* best-seller, former economic hit man (EHM) John Perkins exposes the next phase of a global power play that is re-shaping nations and economies worldwide. With twelve explosive new chapters, Perkins reveals how China has adopted—and adapted—the EHM model, extending its reach across Latin America, Asia, Africa, the Middle East, and Europe.

Perkins delivers a rare insider account of a corrupt system that uses development loans and massive infrastructure deals to trap countries in crushing debt, extracting political leverage, strategic resources, and long-term control. Once associated primarily with US foreign policy, this strategy has entered a new era—one defined by intensifying global competition, staggering income inequality, and accelerating ecological destruction. The result is what Perkins calls a "death economy": a system that prioritizes short-term profits over people and planet.

But this book is not just an exposé—it's a call to action. Perkins outlines a bold and practical path forward, urging a shift toward a "life economy" that values sustainability, shared prosperity, and genuine international cooperation. He challenges readers to recognize their own power in shaping a more just and regenerative global system. The stakes have never been higher—and the opportunity for change has never been more urgent.

Berrett-Koehler

PUBLISHERS

Dear Reader,

Welcome to the Berrett-Koehler Community—a global network of changemakers creating positive impact in their lives, organizations, and communities.

Our Mission: Connecting People and Ideas to Create a World That Works for All

We believe transformation is possible. While outdated paradigms of self-interest, exclusion, and hierarchy continue to hold back our communities and organizations, we know that change can happen. That's why we connect people with actionable ideas from leading experts who are already creating the solutions we need.

The BK Way

We're an independent publisher that practices what we publish. Our books, digital resources, and community offerings provide practical pathways for building more just, equitable, and sustainable organizations and lives. Whether you're transforming your workplace, community, or personal practices, our publications meet you where you are with tools that work.

But we don't just talk about positive change—we live it. Through "The BK Way," we put stewardship and purpose before profit. As a benefit corporation, we're legally committed to benefiting all our stakeholders: authors, readers, employees, communities, and the environment.

As our gift to you, claim your free bestselling ebook at bkconnection.com/welcome. You'll also receive fresh leadership insights delivered to your inbox from bkconnection.com/blogs/the-bk-exchange.

You Make the Difference

We're grateful to our readers, authors, and community members, who bring our mission to life every day. Your stories of transformation inspire us and show others what's possible.

Share how BK publications are making a difference in your world at bkconnection.com/impact.

Your friends at Berrett-Koehler

Join the Berrett-Koehler Community

Are you passionate about supporting independent publishing and reading diverse voices and perspectives? Join the BK Community Membership Program and become a part of a vibrant literary community. To support mission-based publishing while saving up to 30 percent on all books and attending exclusive events, visit ideas.bkconnection.com/bkcommunity-join to learn more and become a member.

FSC
www.fsc.org
MIX
Paper | Supporting responsible forestry
FSC® C005010